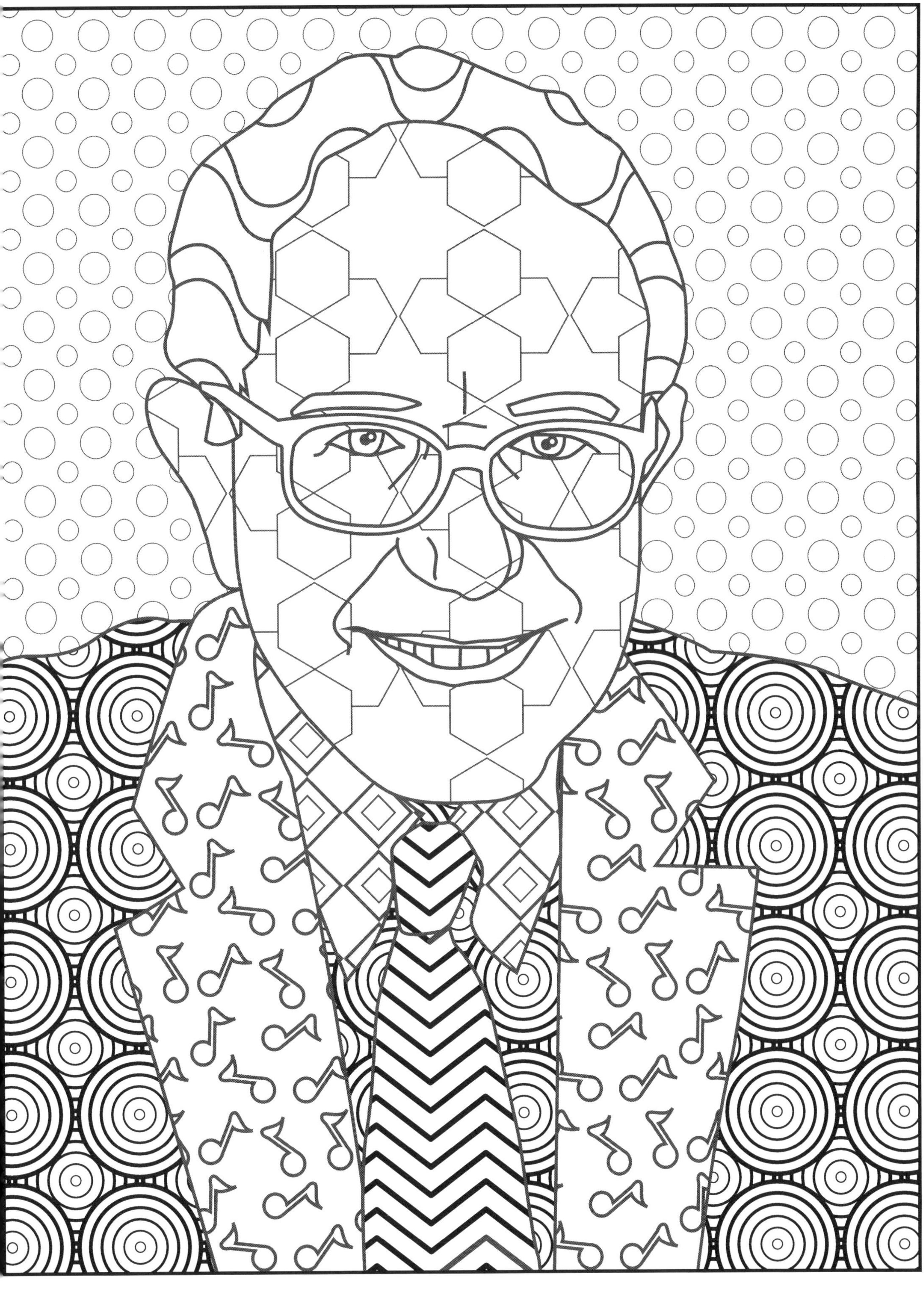

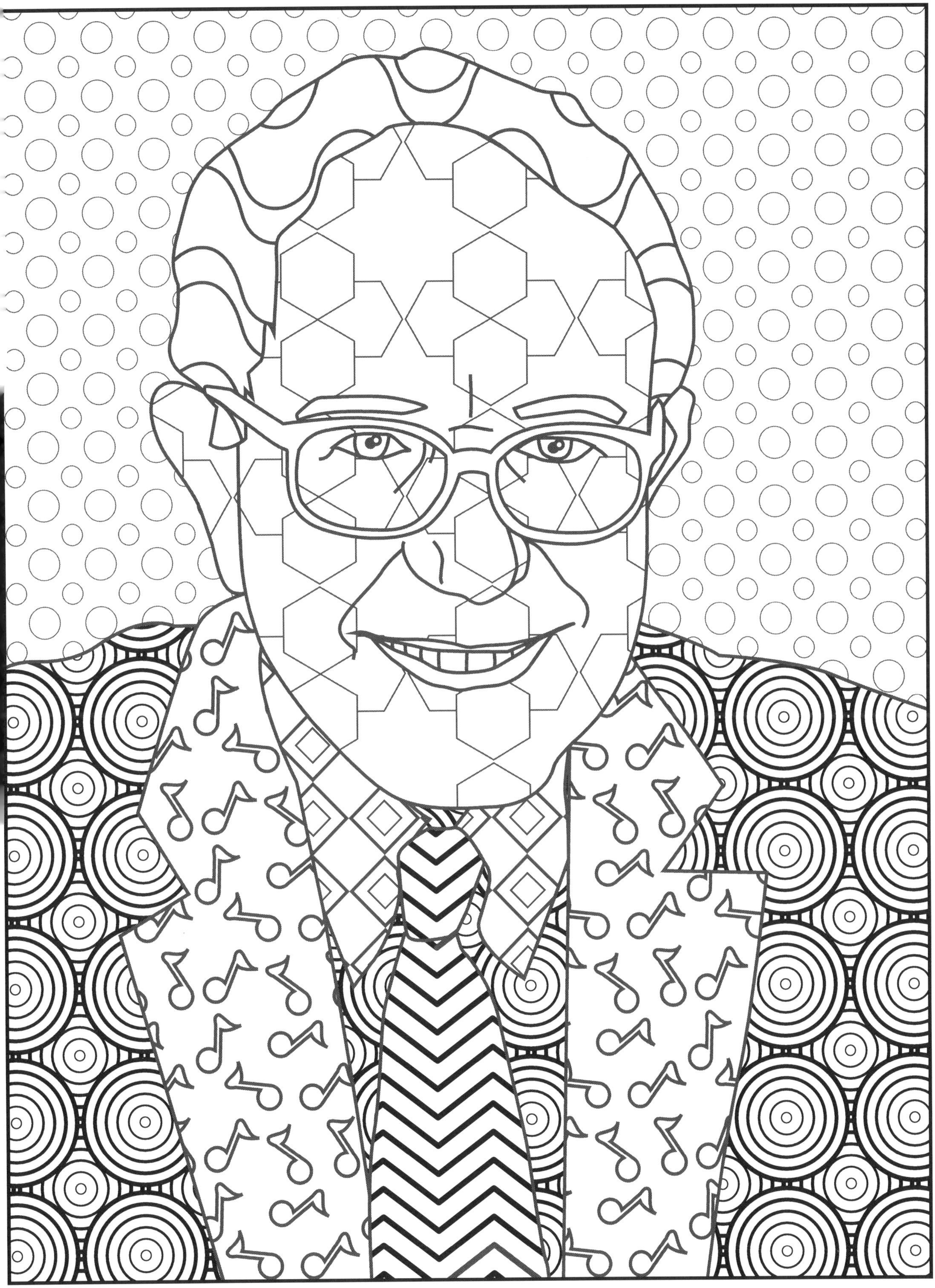

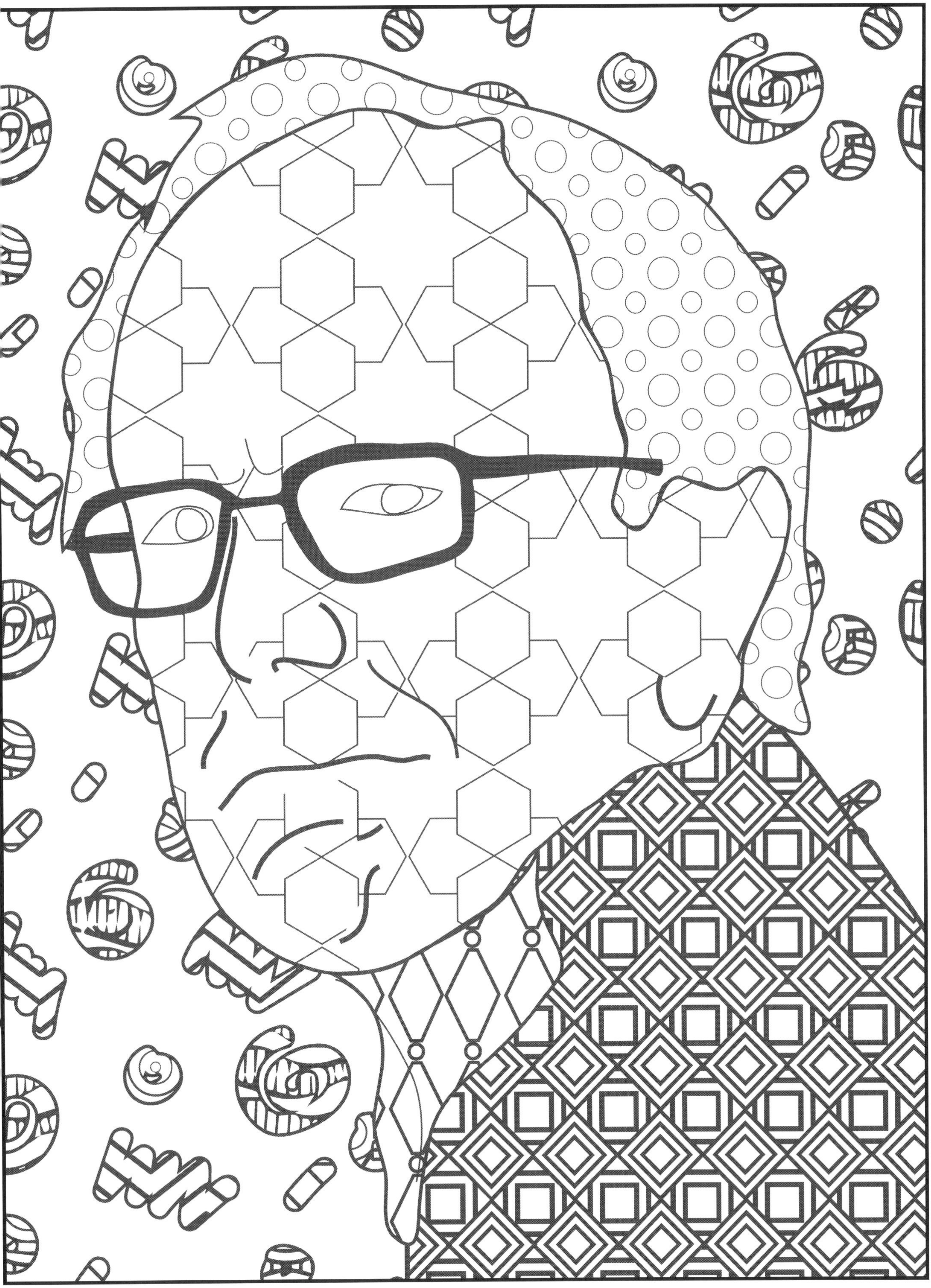

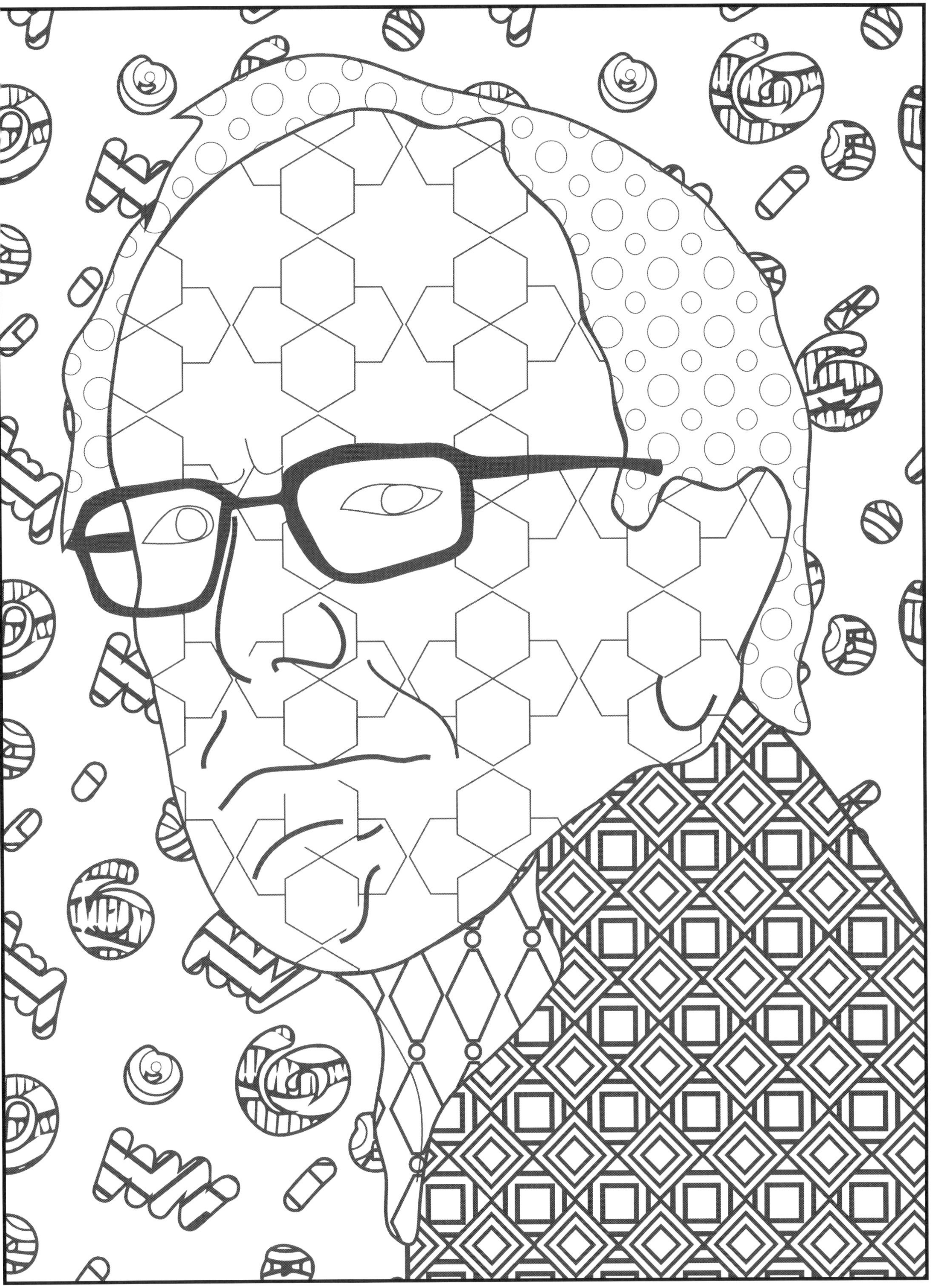

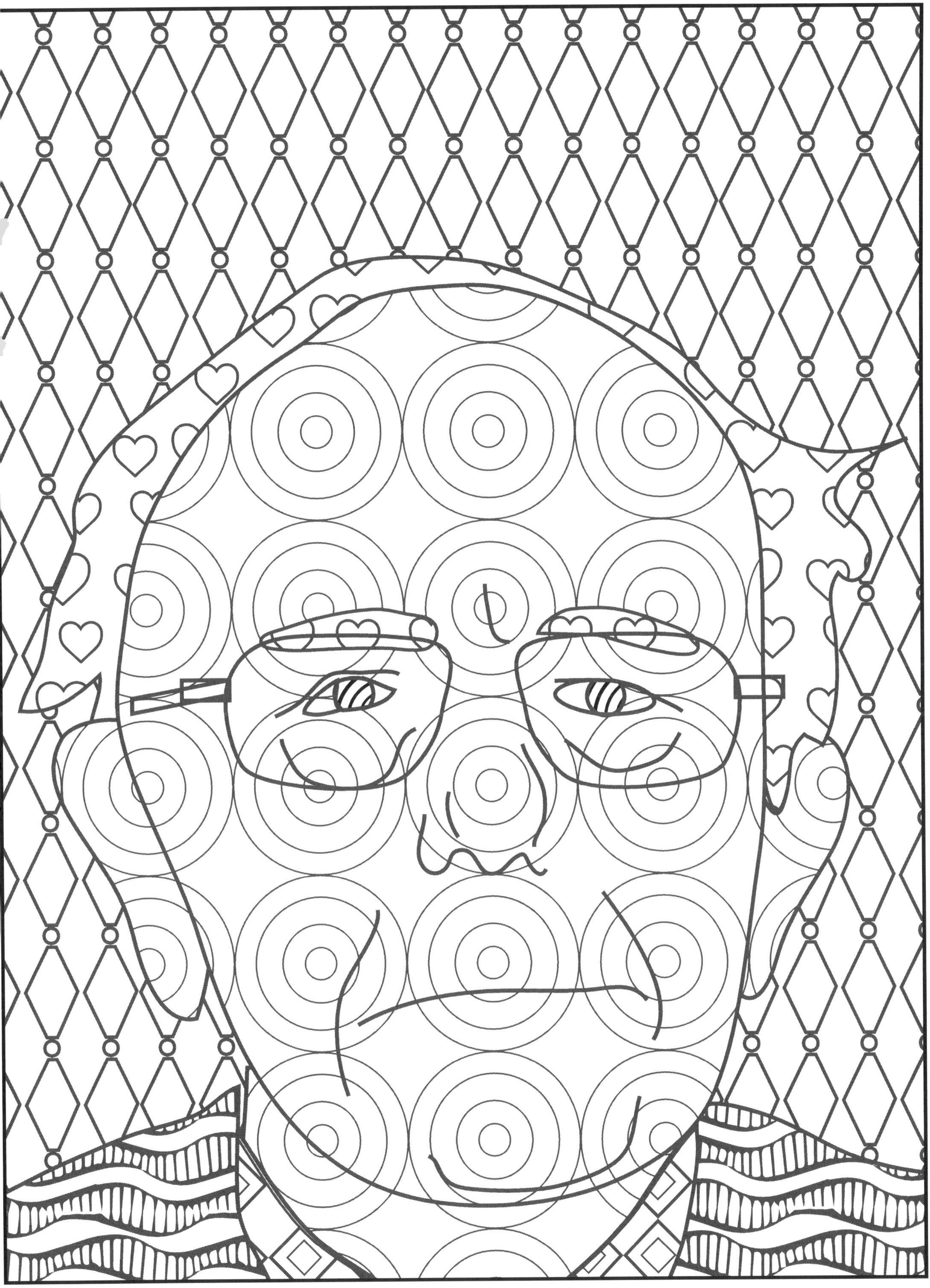

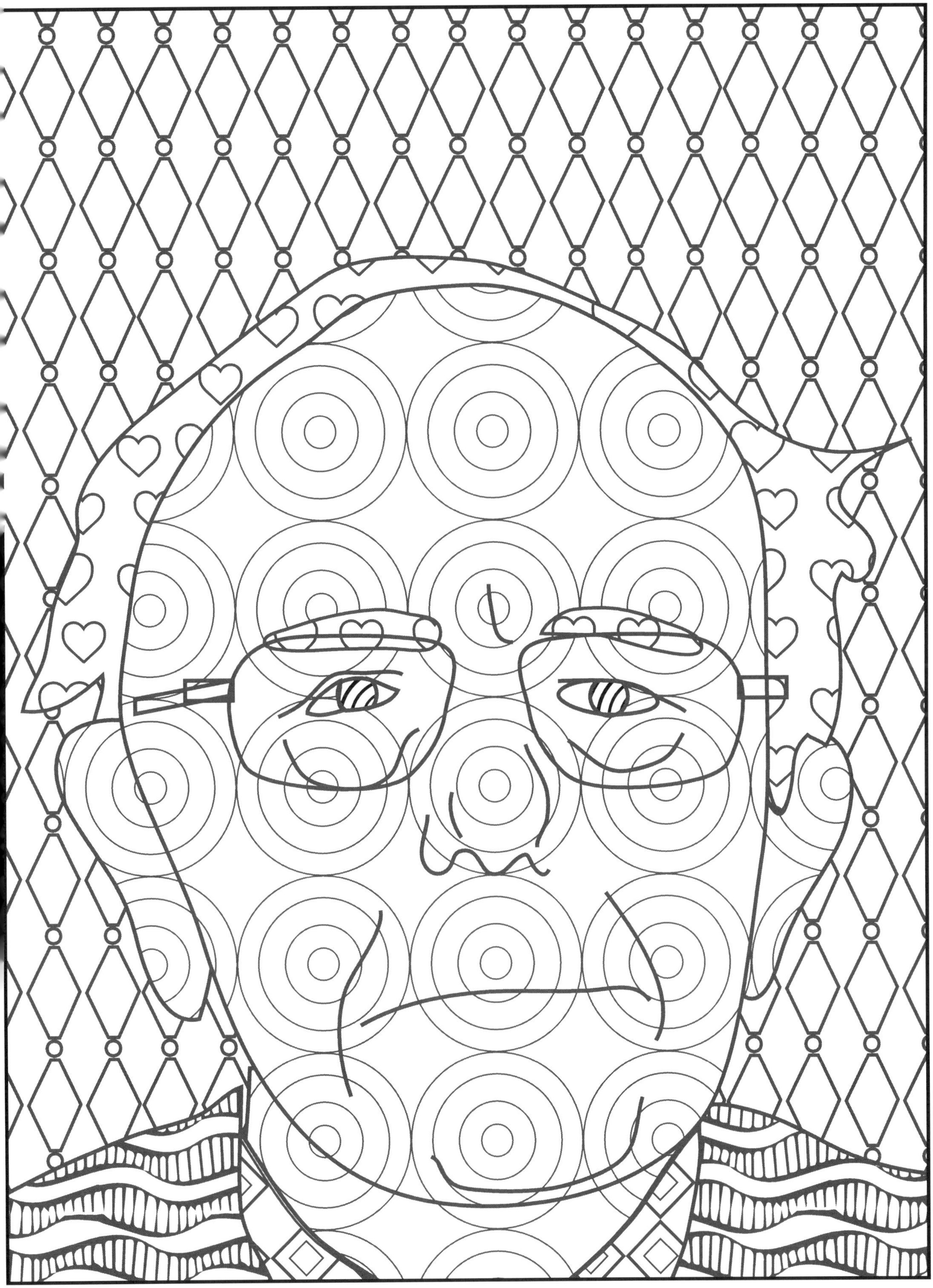

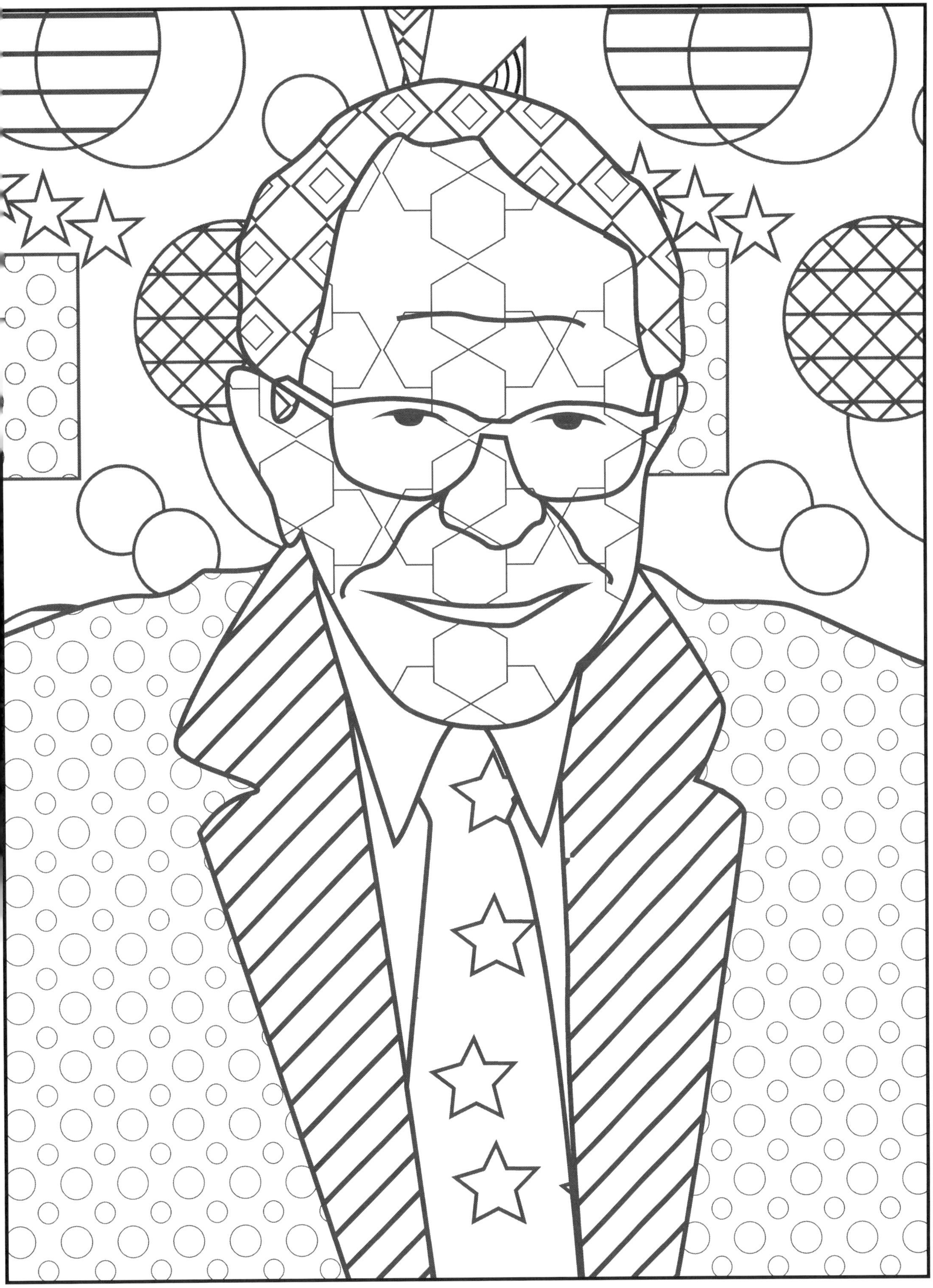

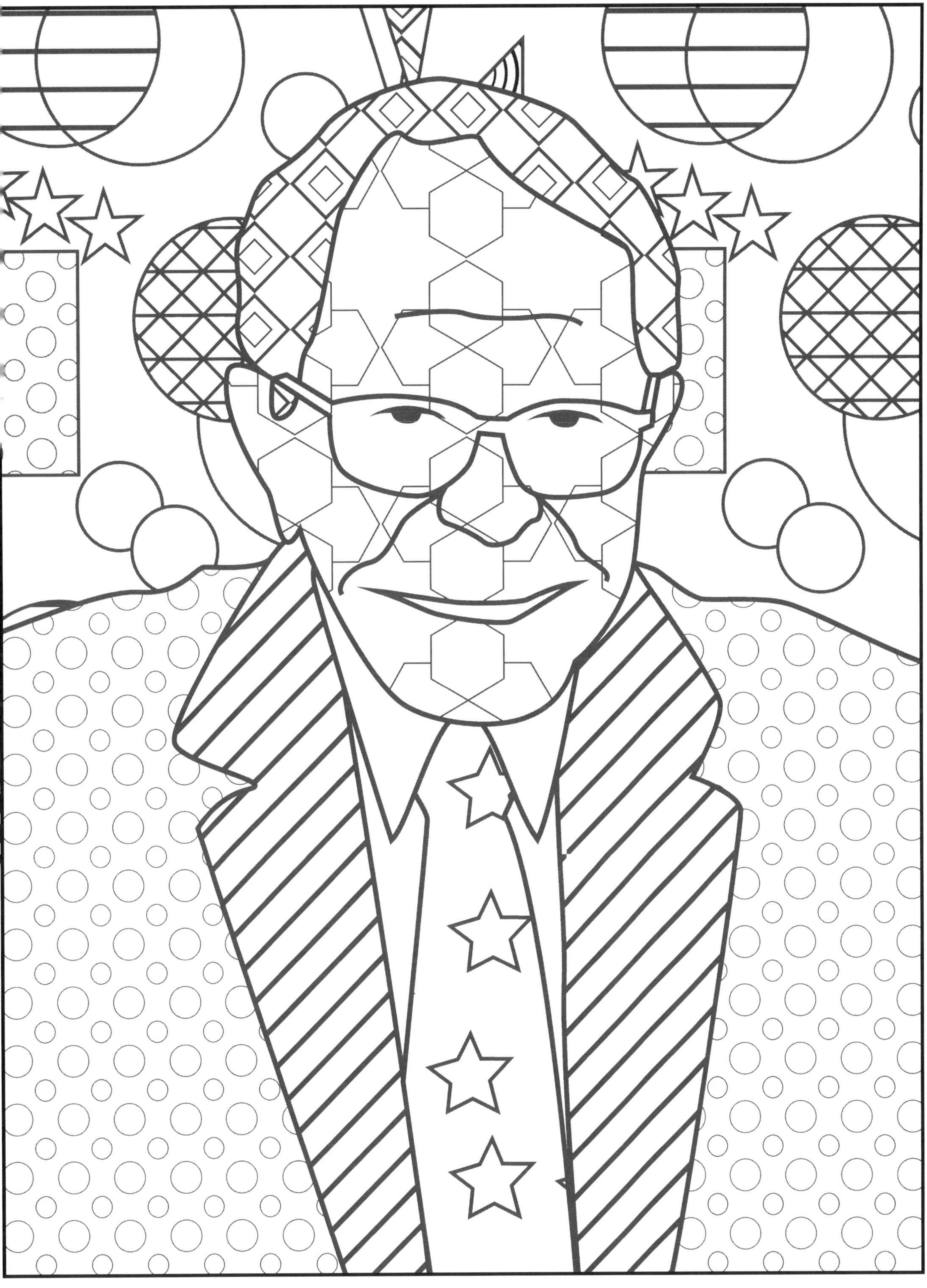

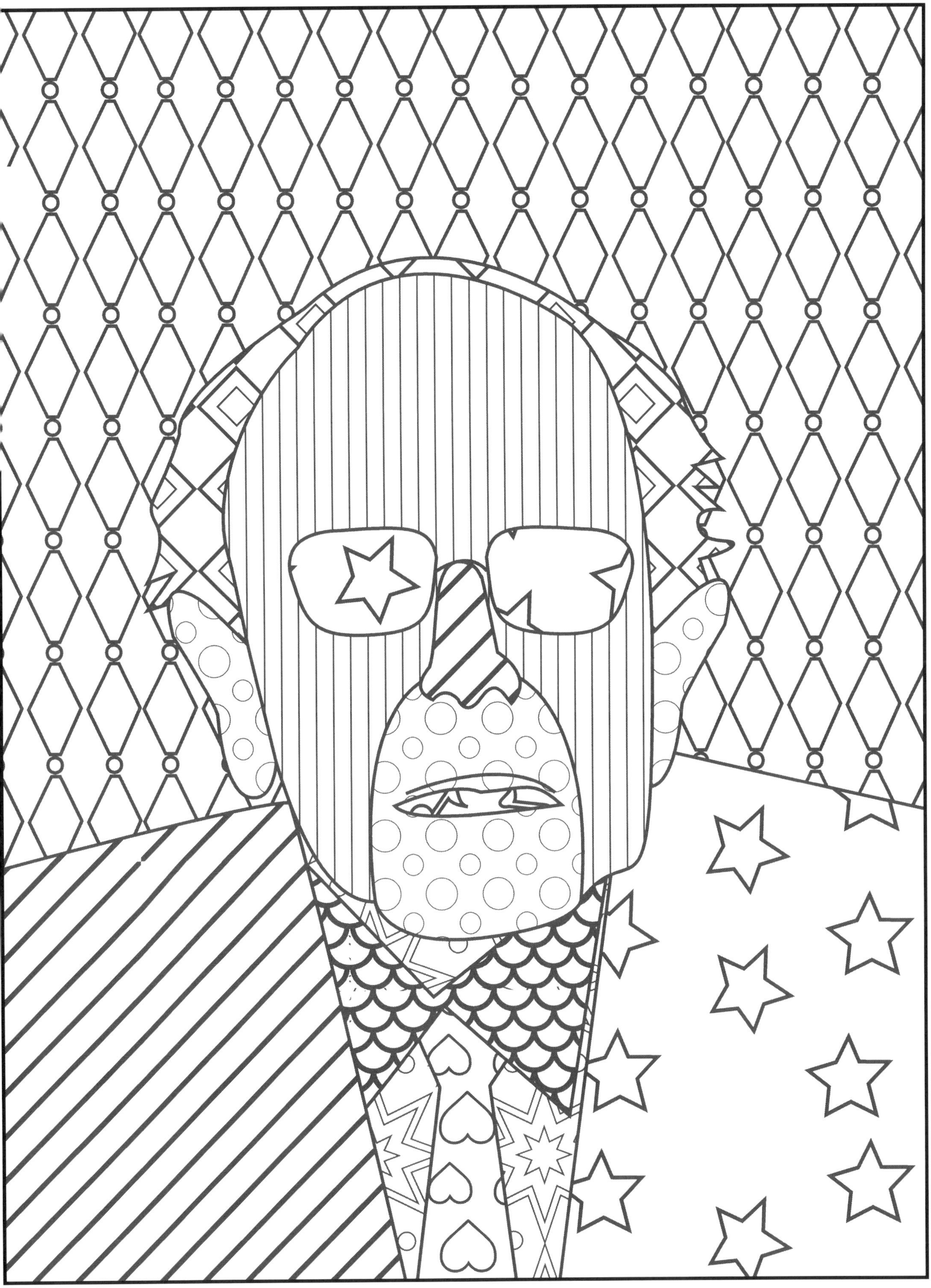

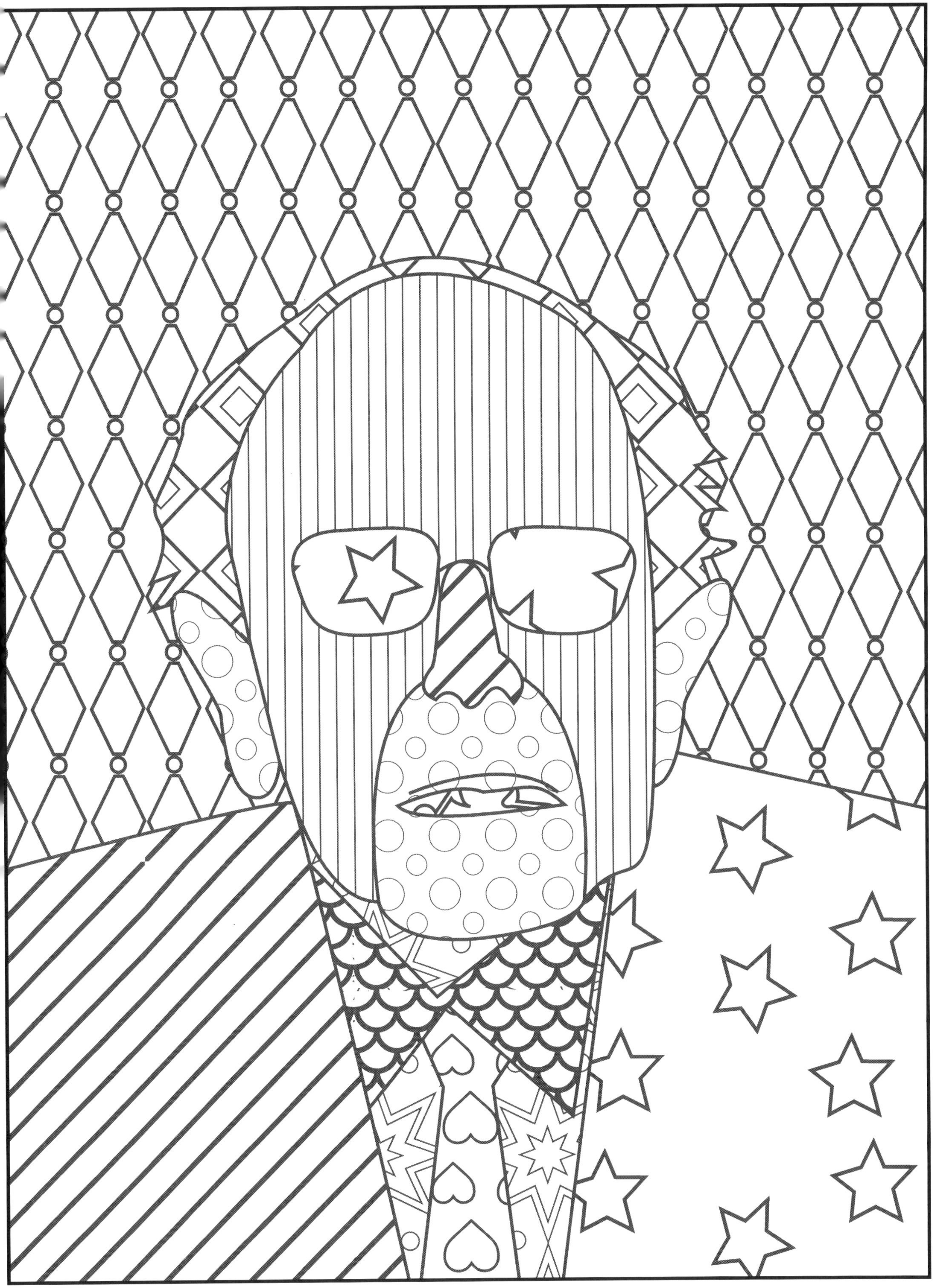

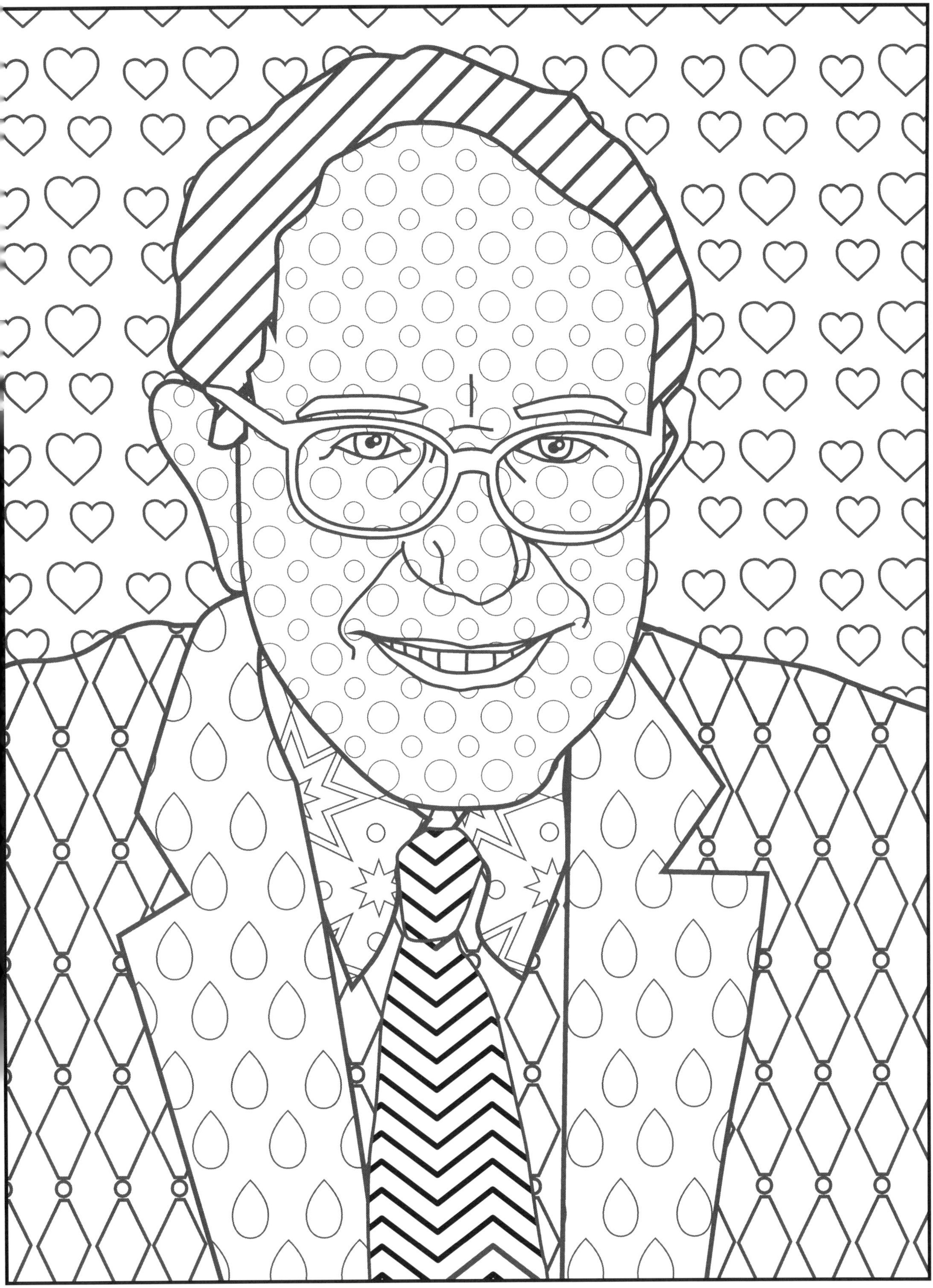

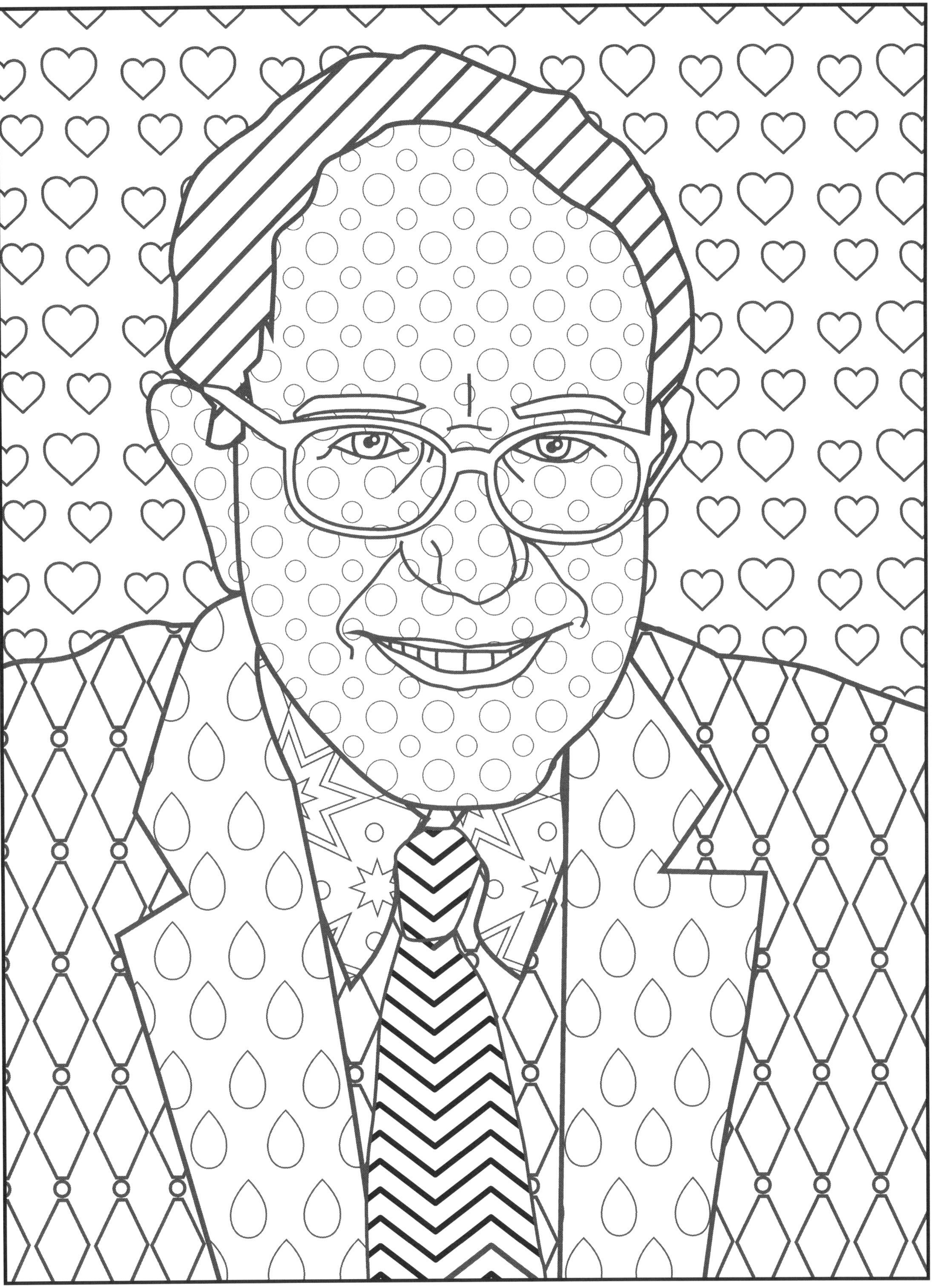

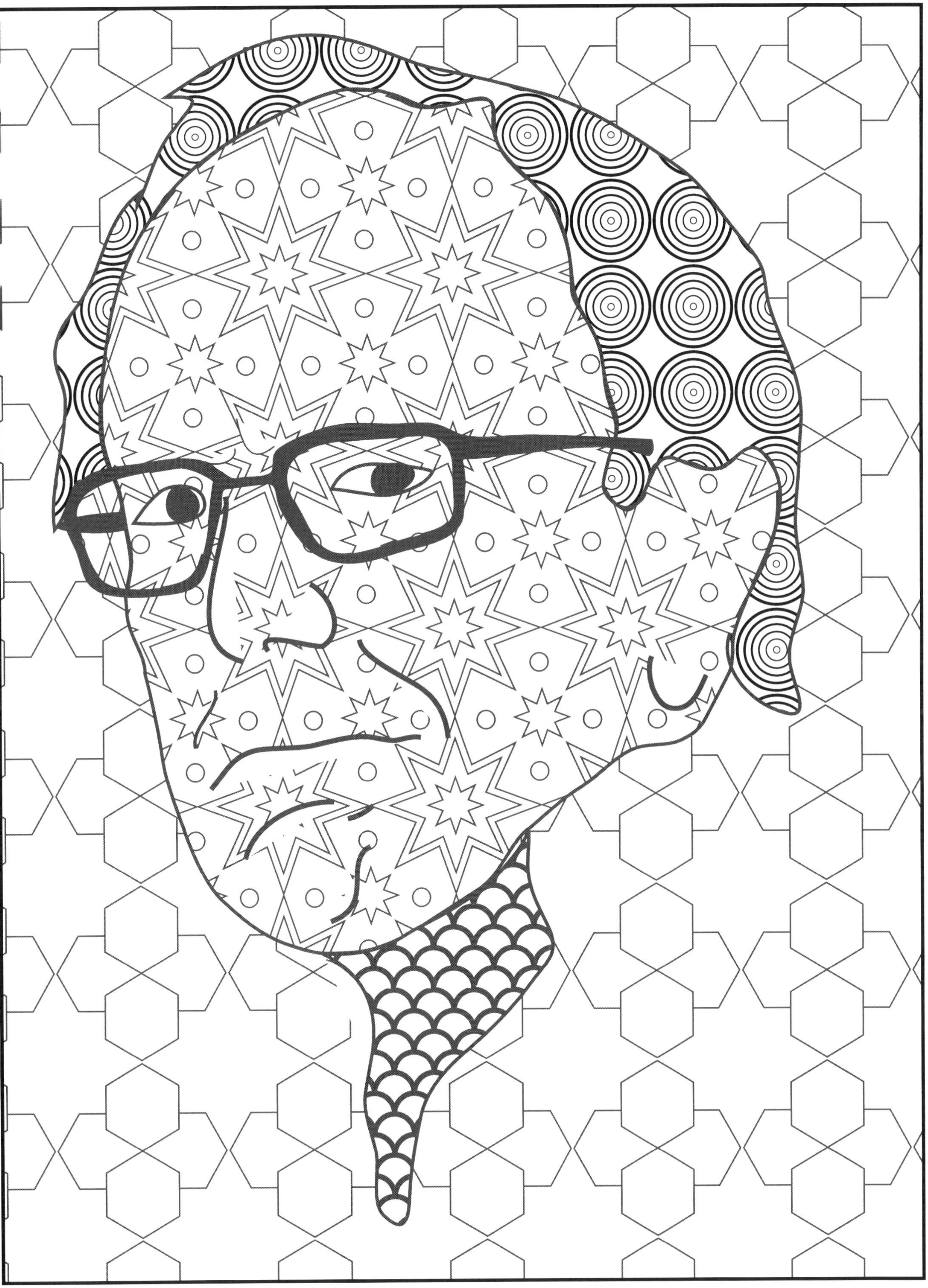

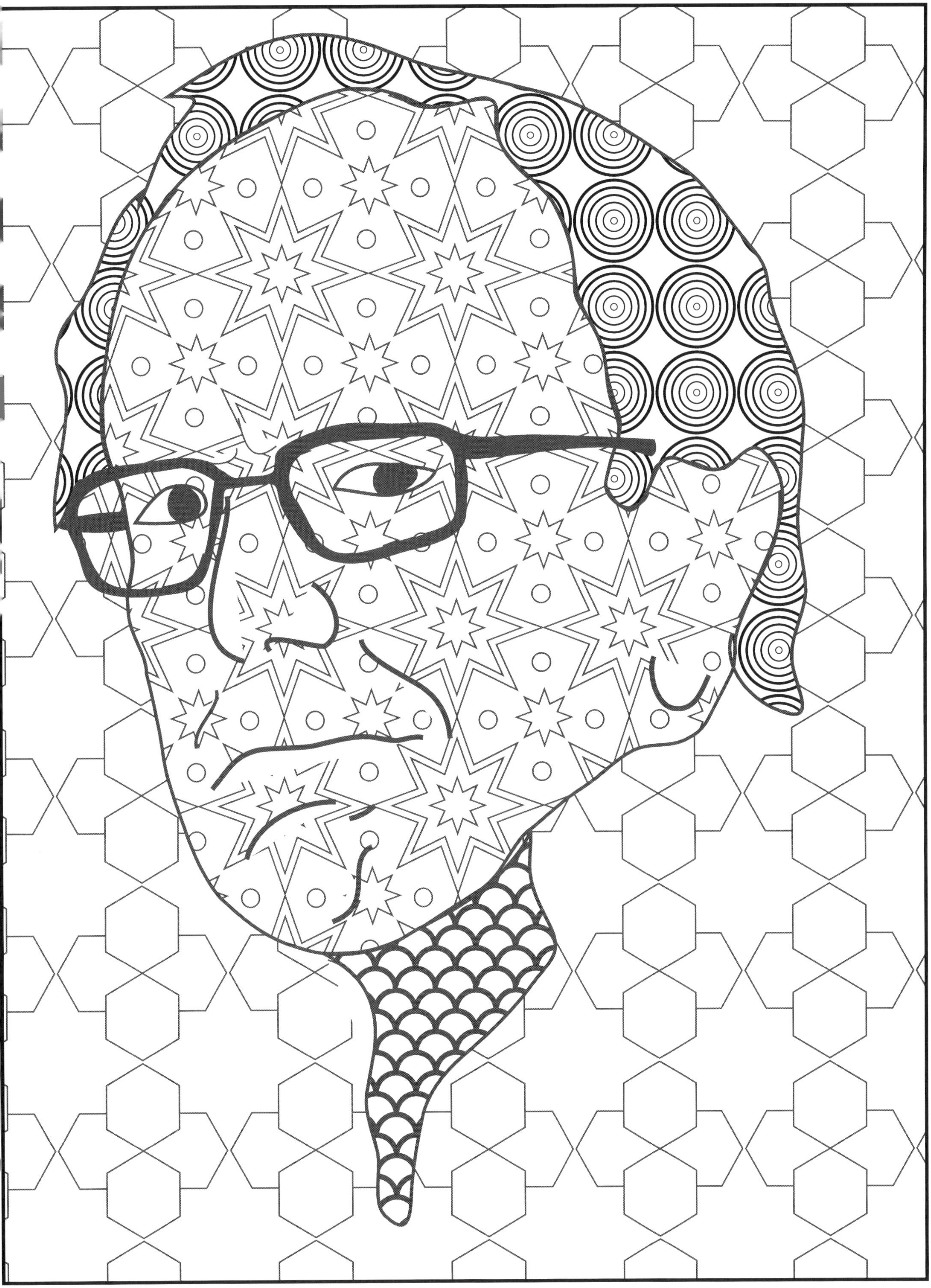

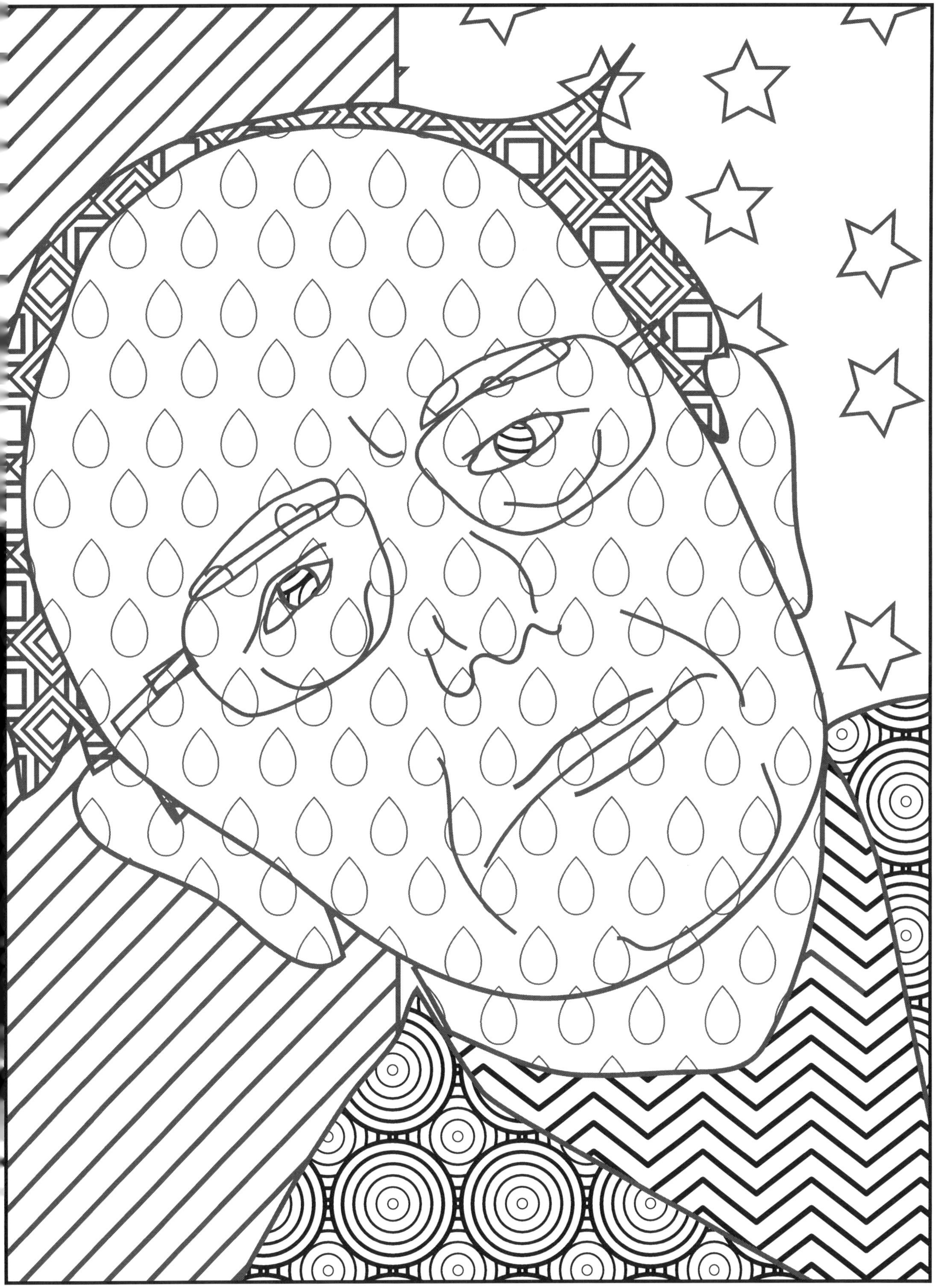

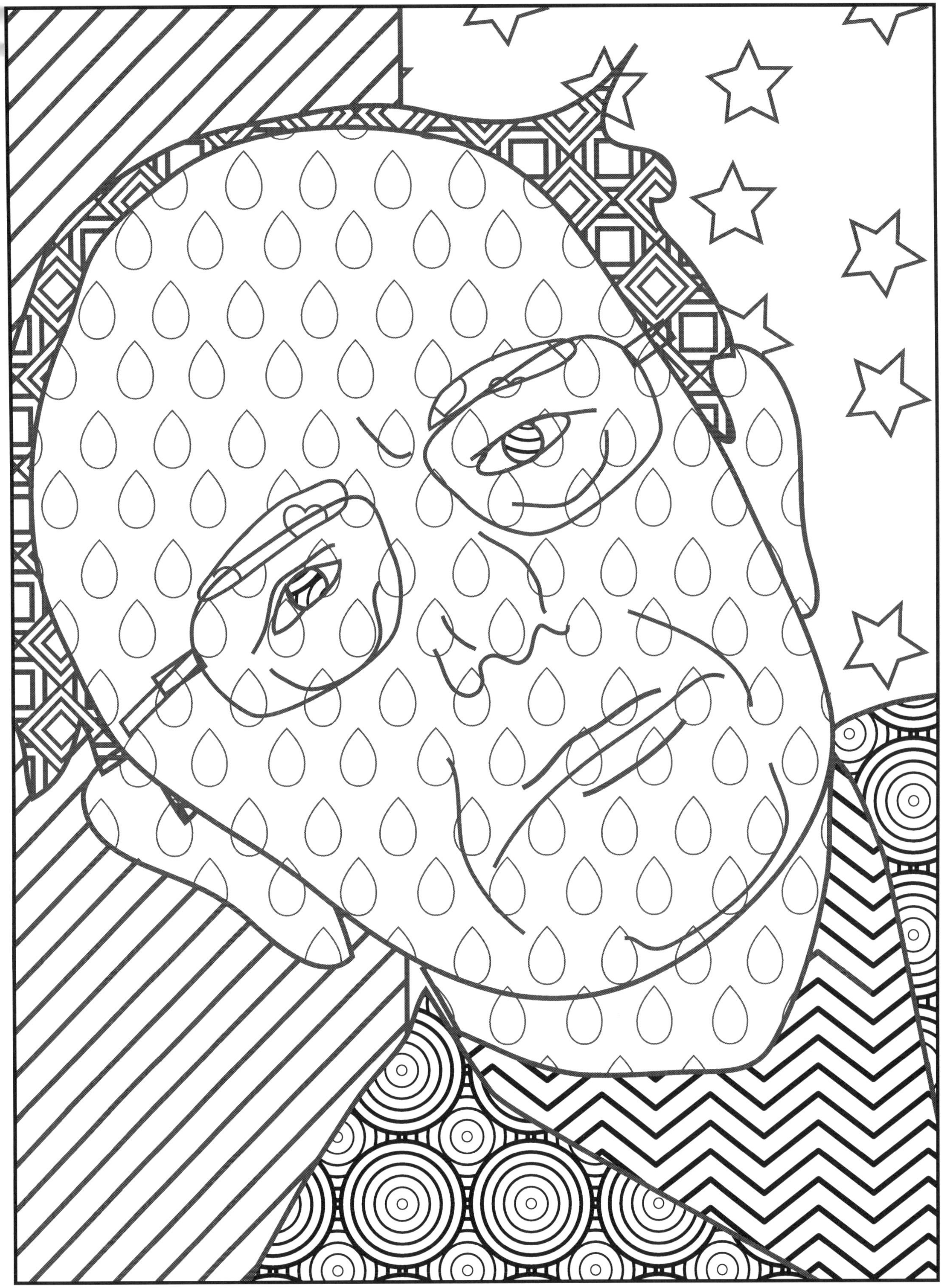

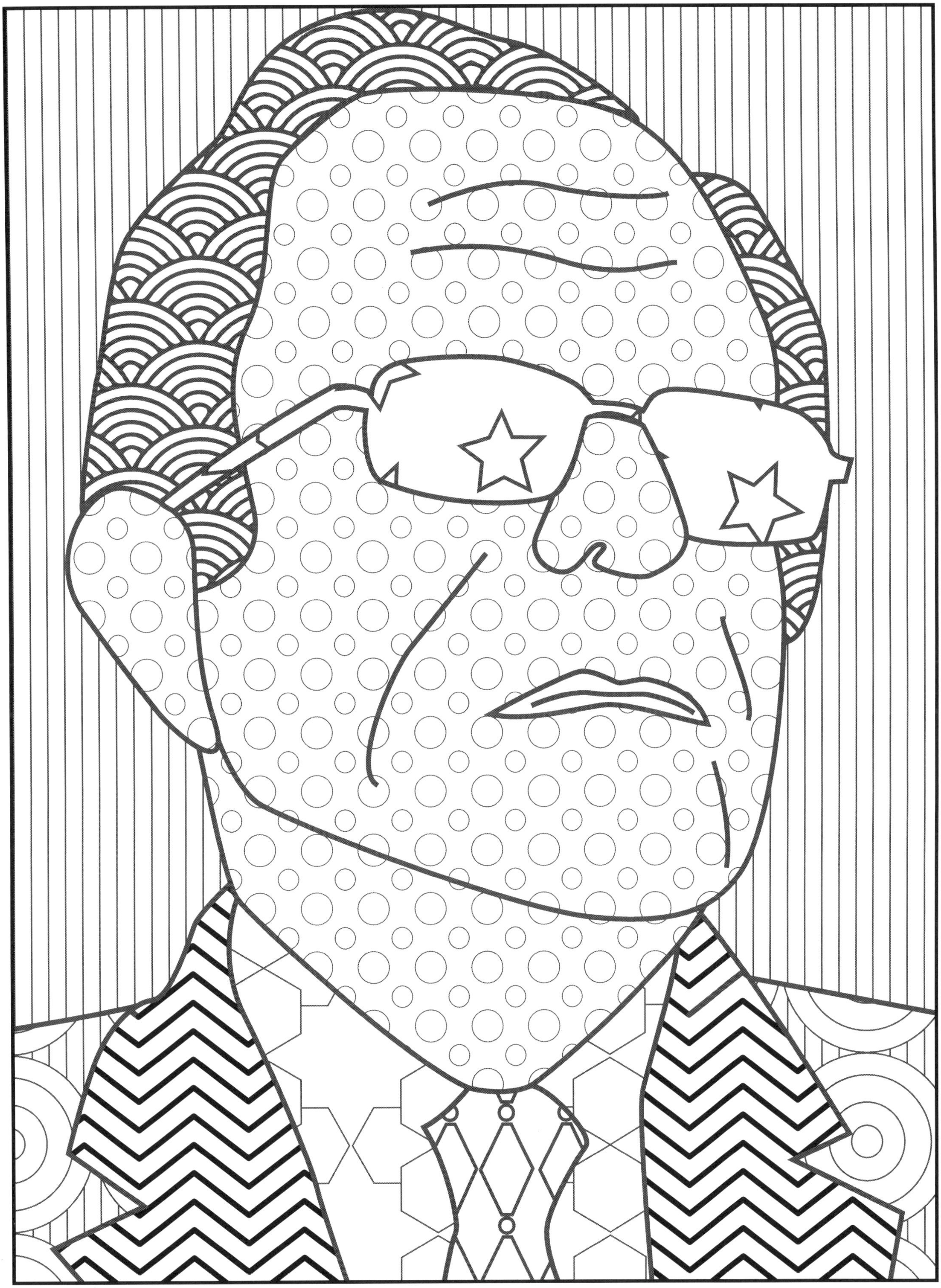

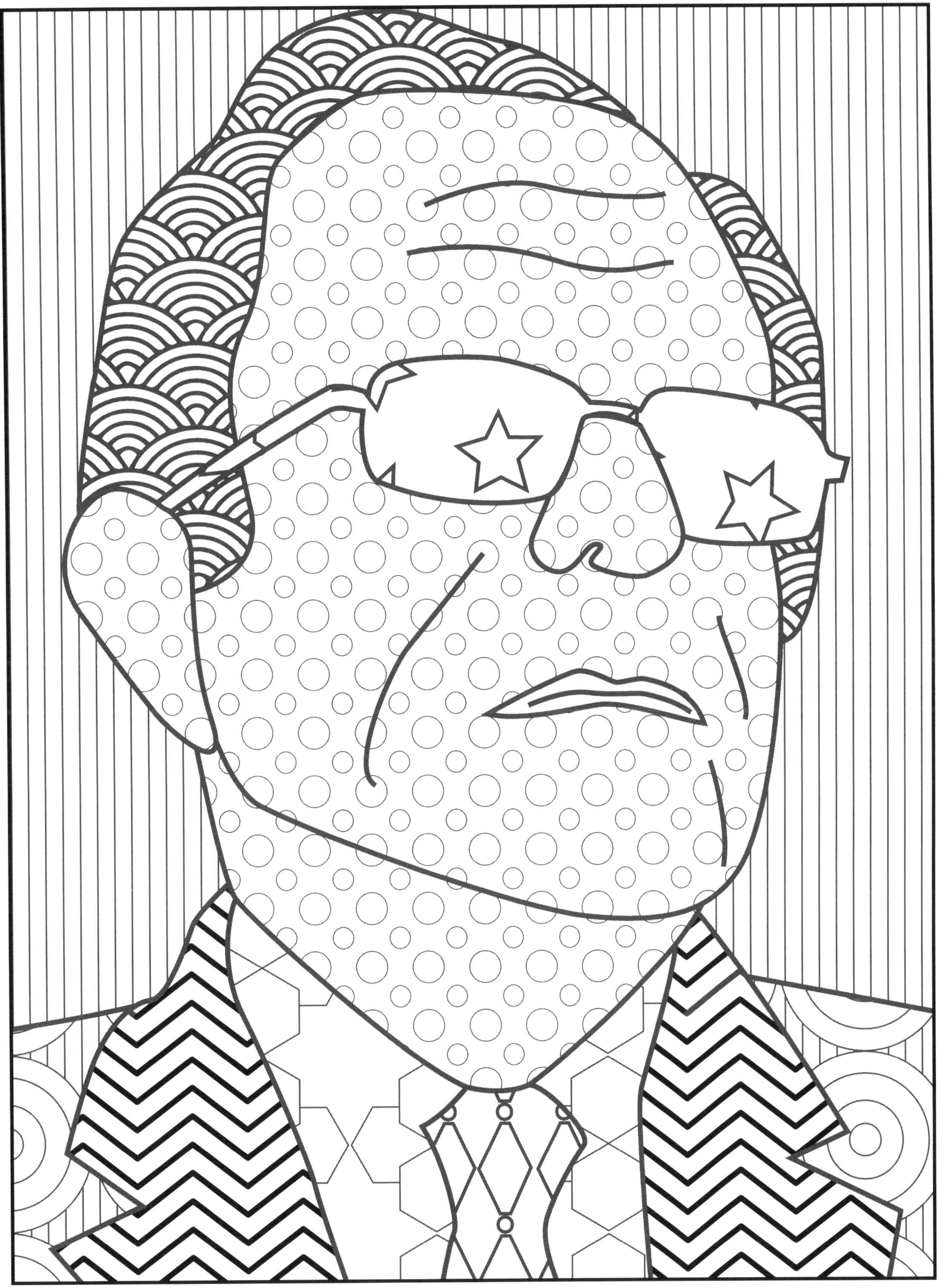

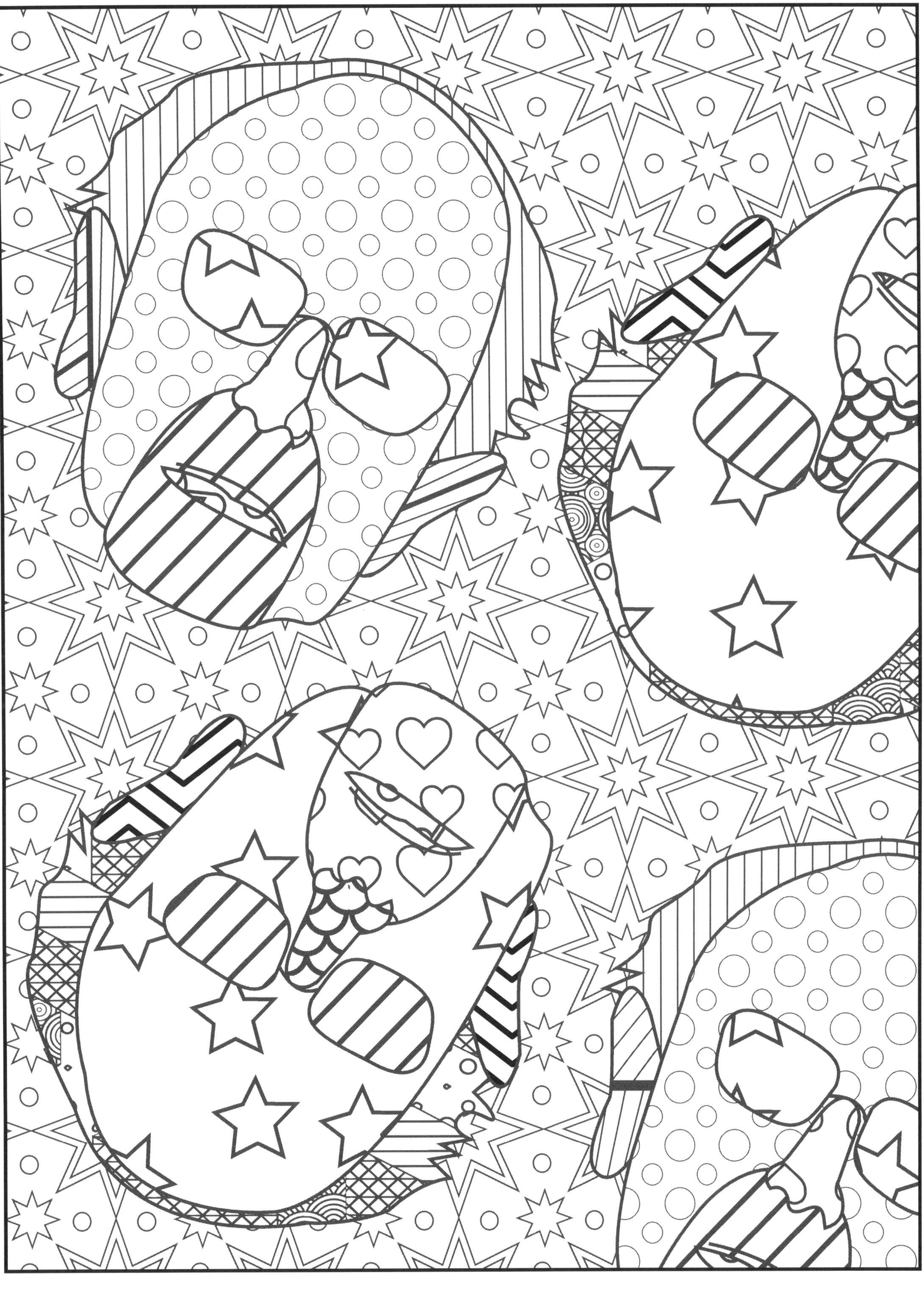

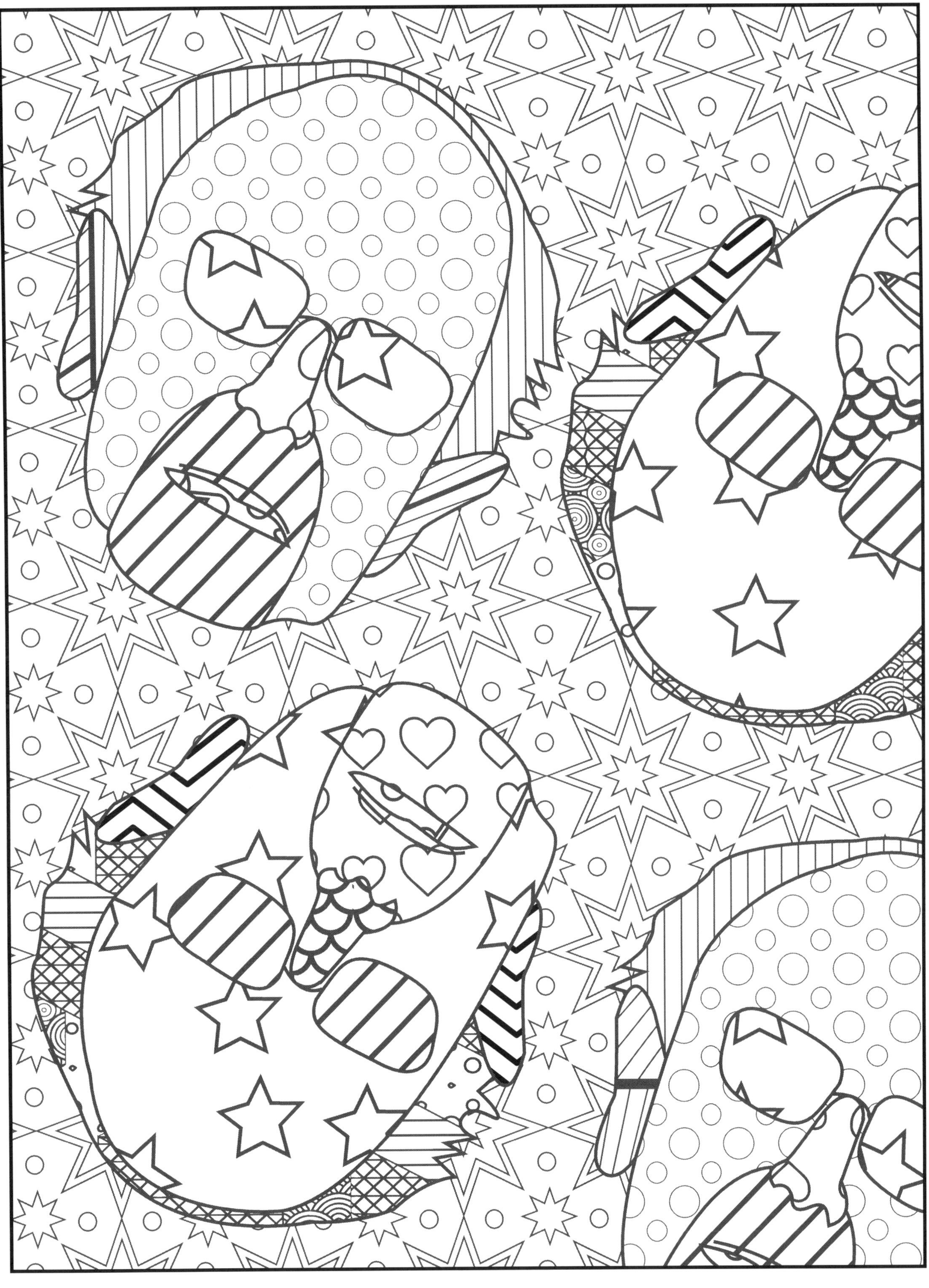

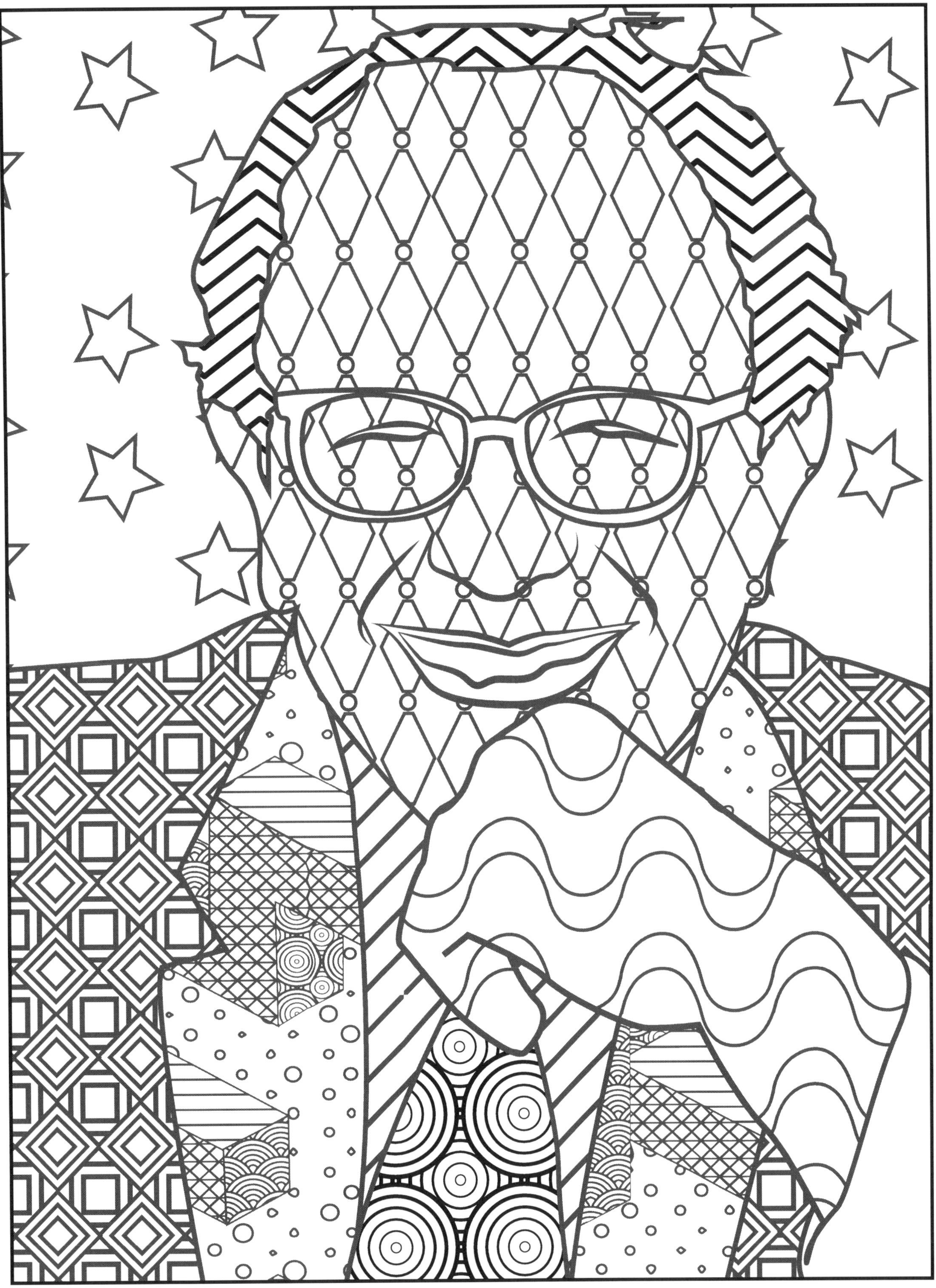

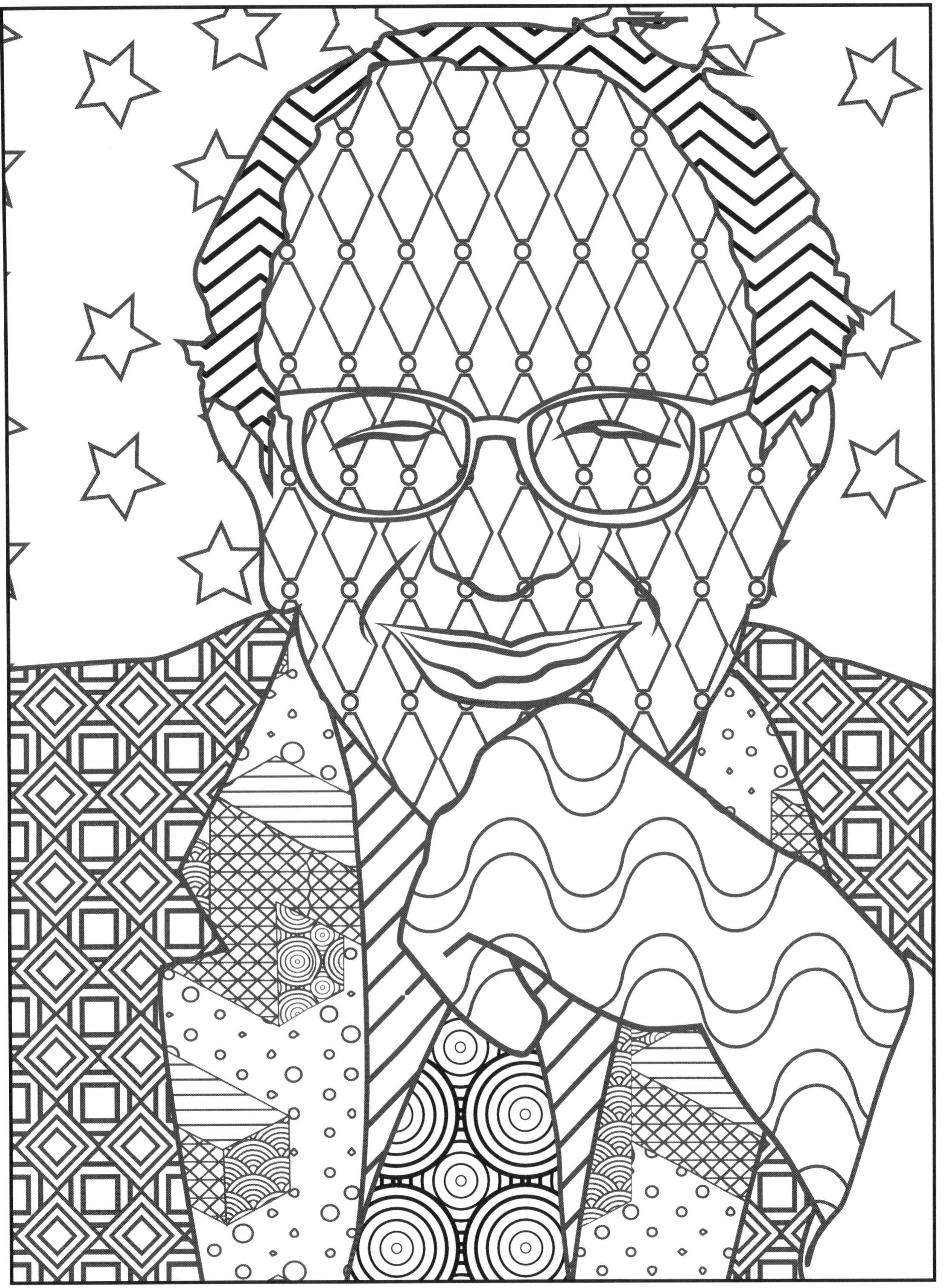

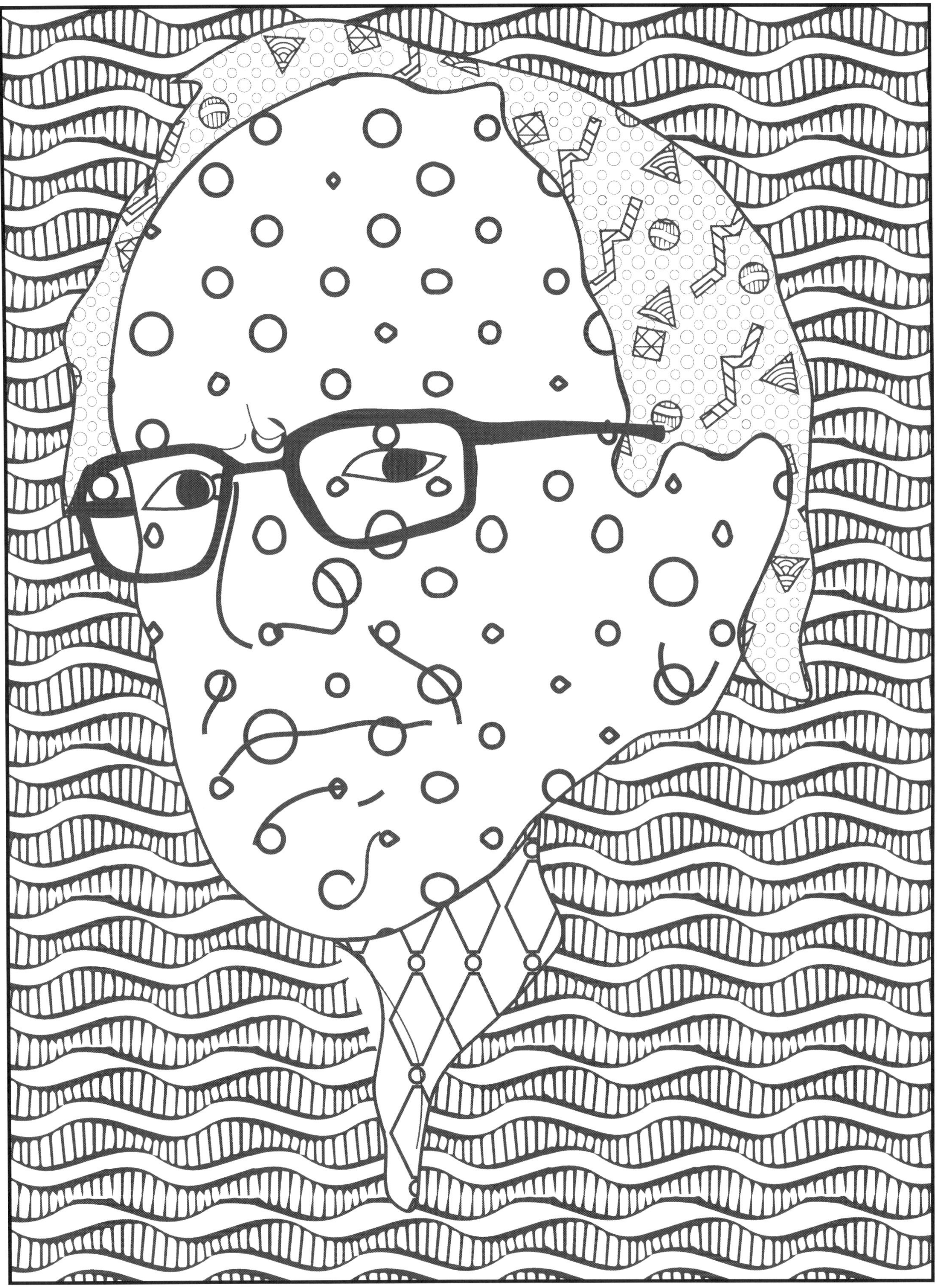

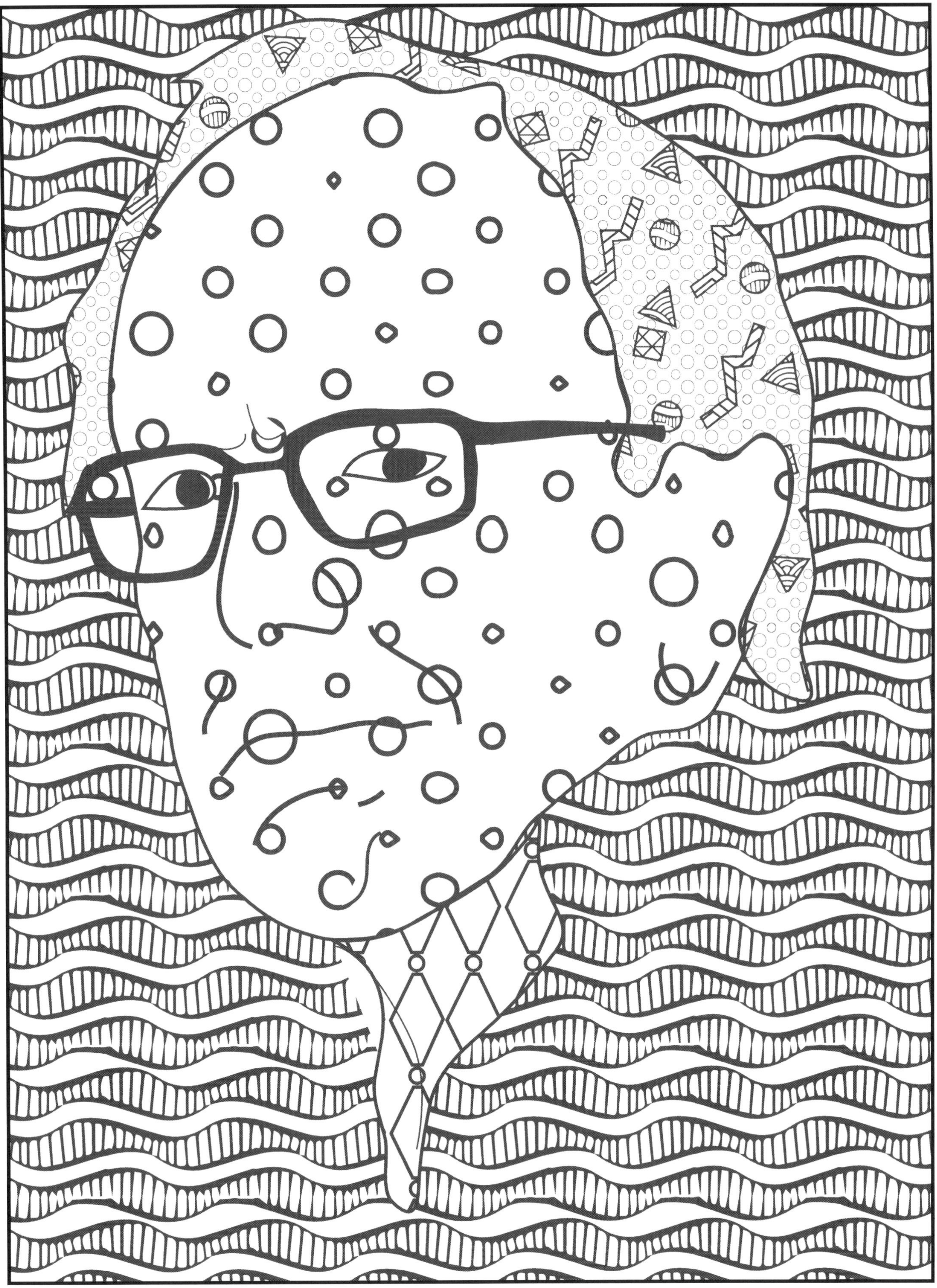

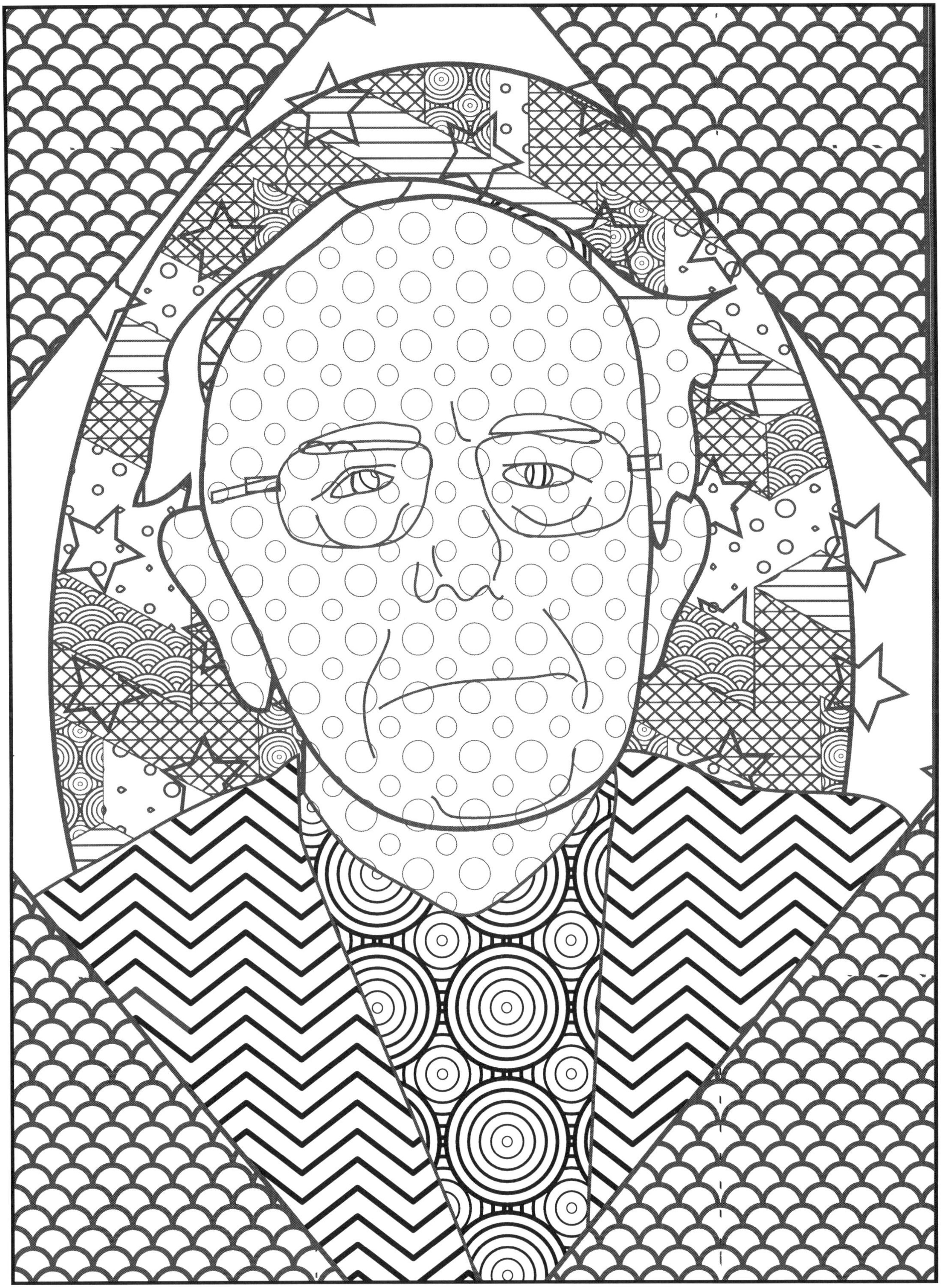

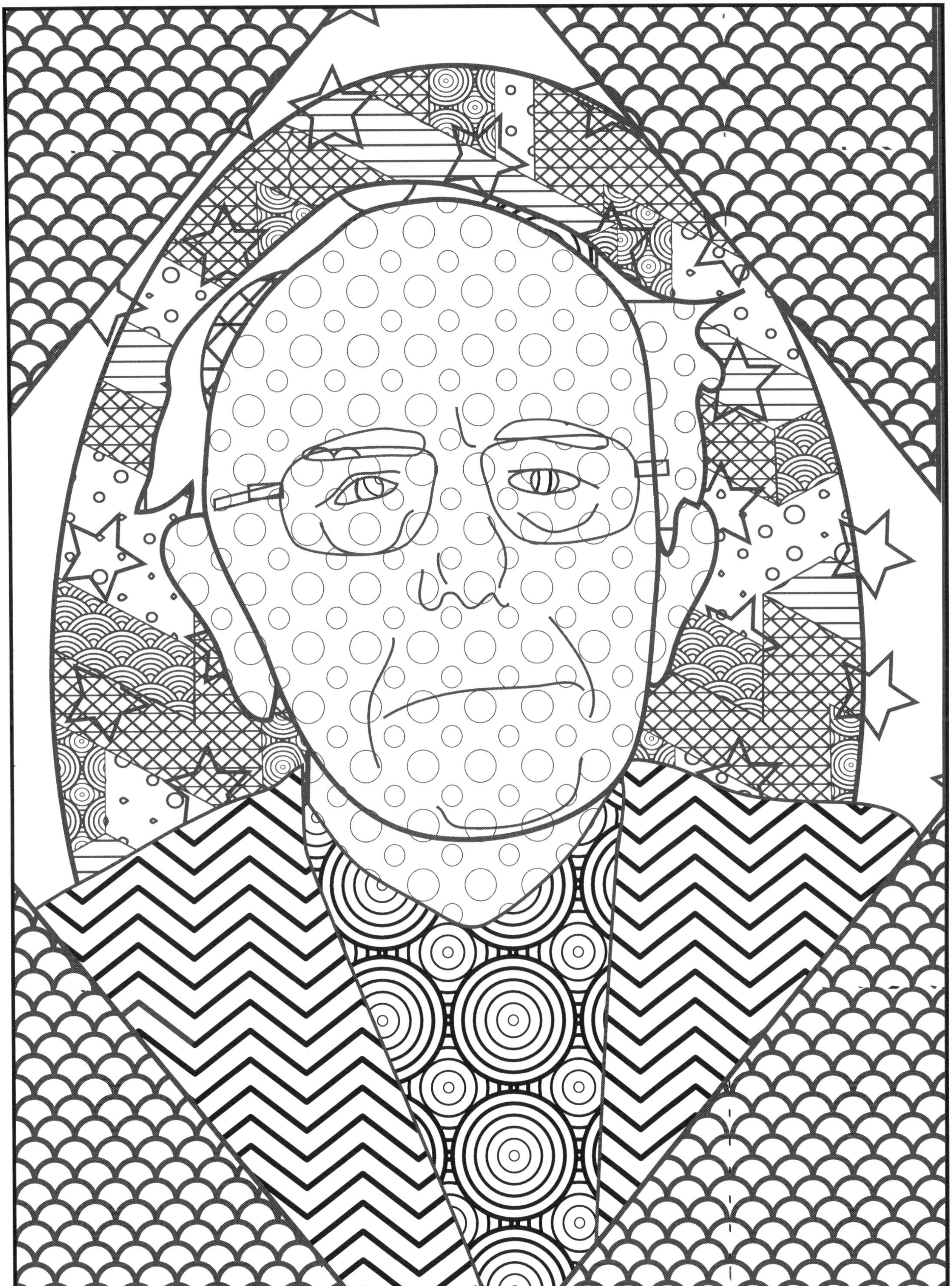

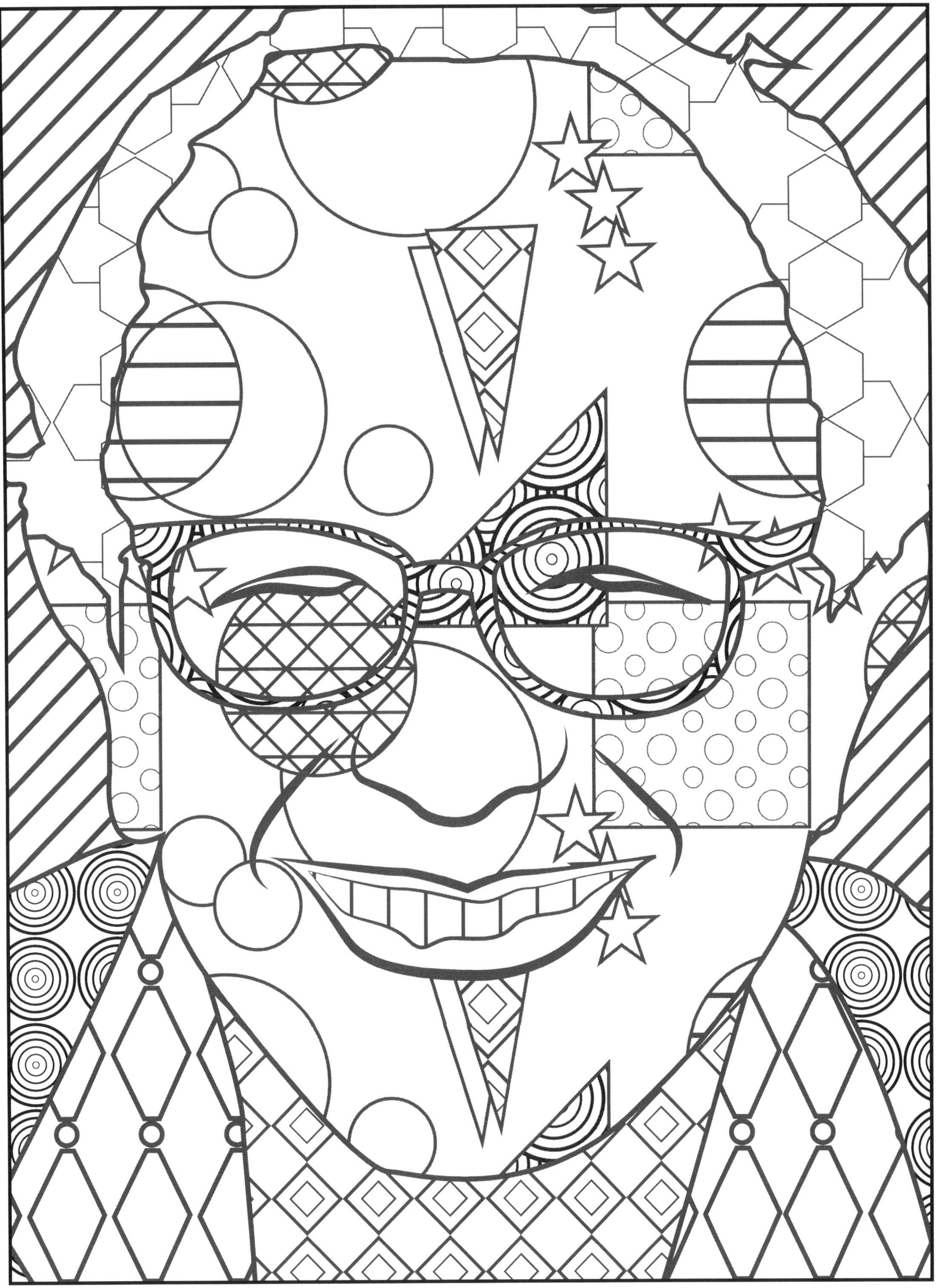

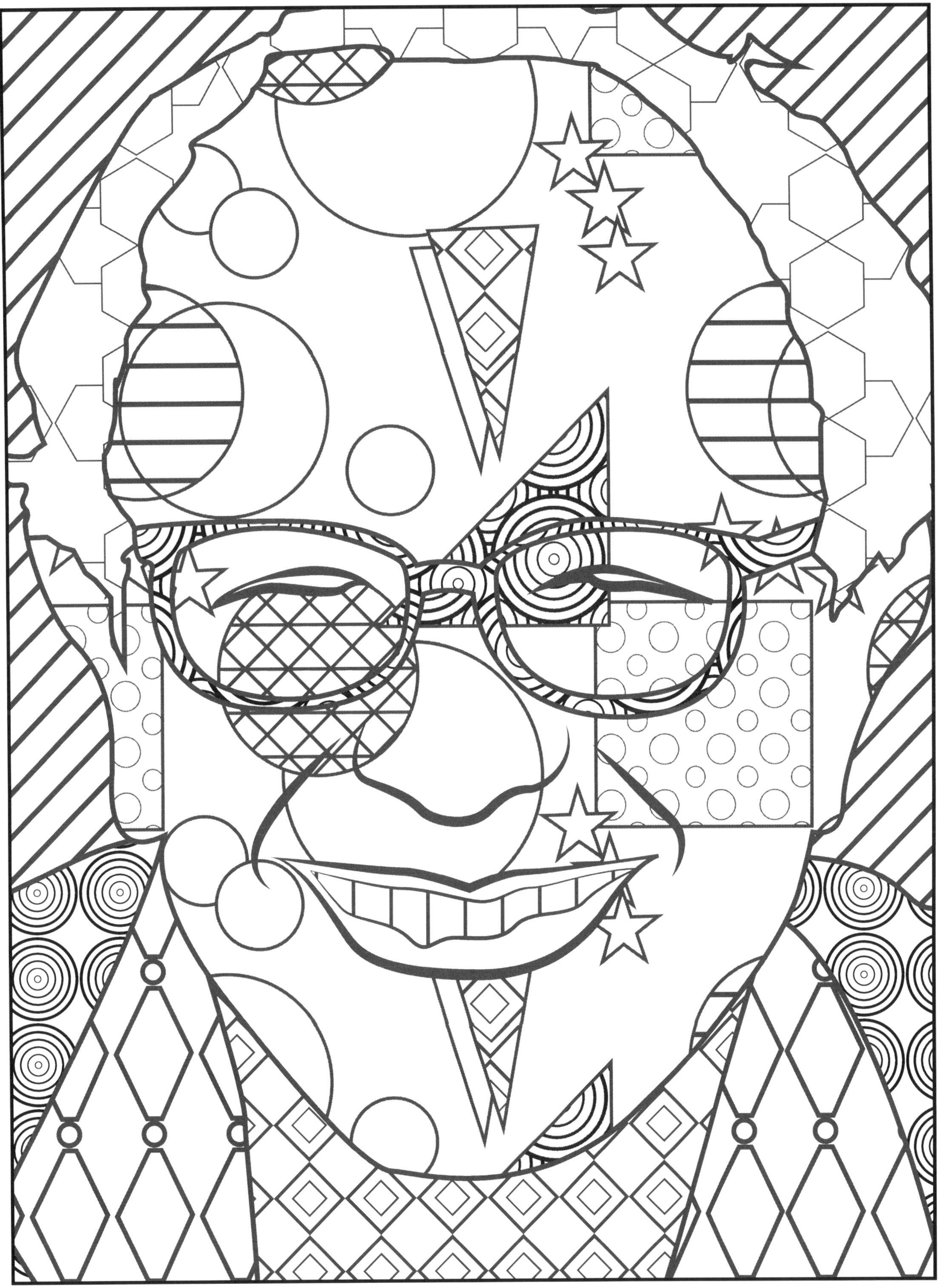

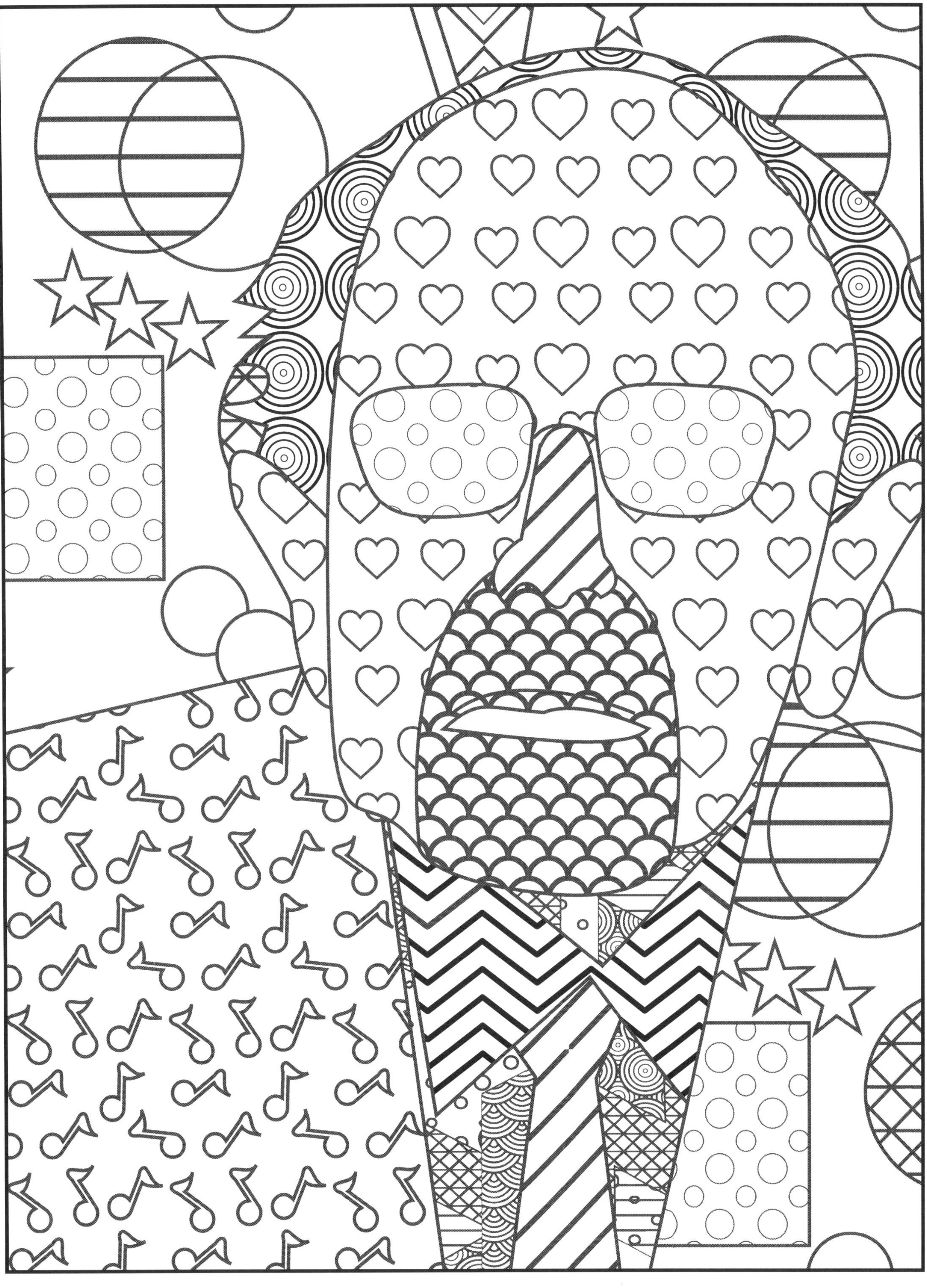

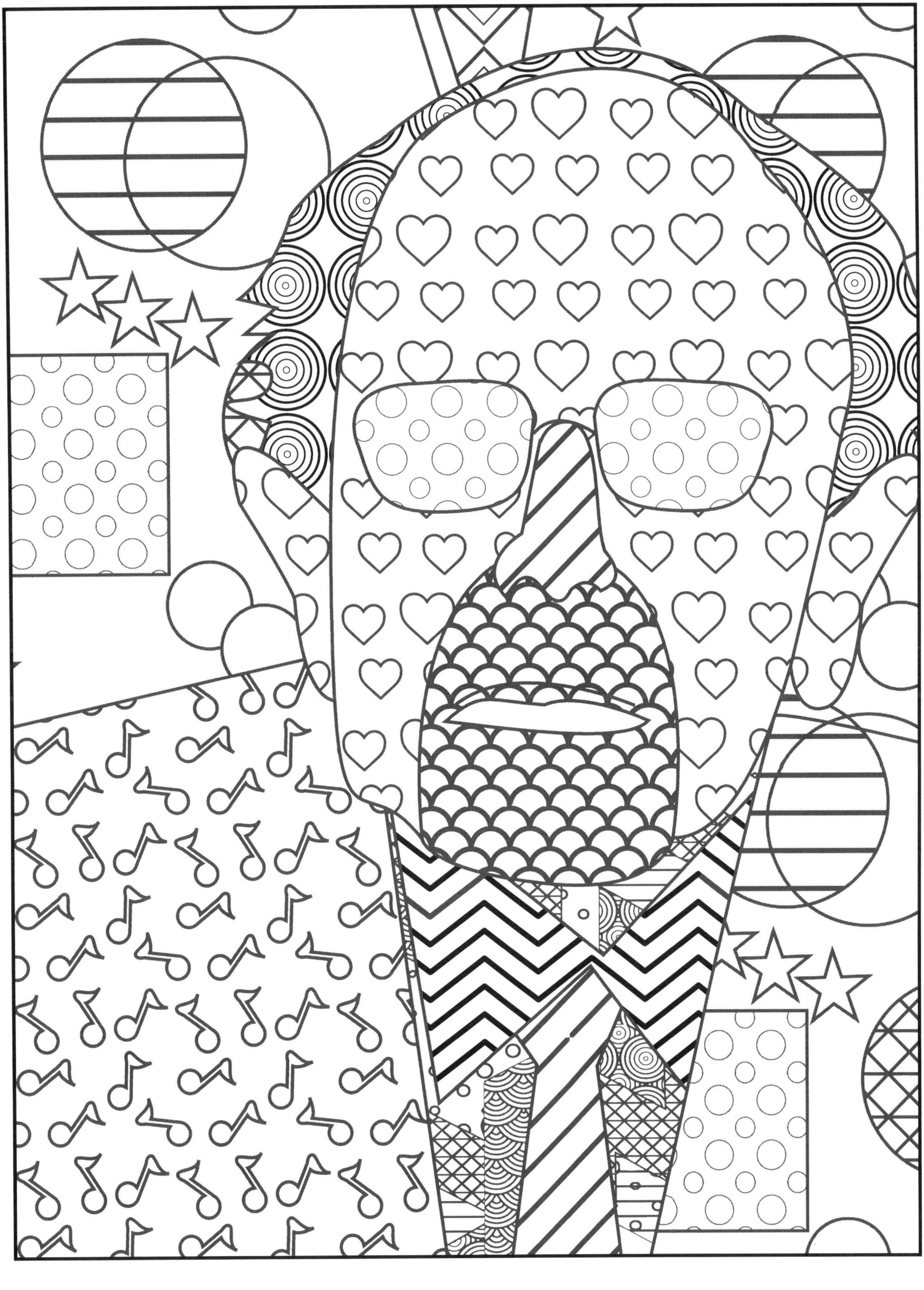

Manufactured by Amazon.ca
Bolton, ON

13742115R00037